Shift Happens!

The Main Thing is to

KEEP the Main Thing

THE MAIN THING

Written by

Jewel Diamond Taylor

2008

Revised 2009

Photography by Teri Williams

e-mail - newlife100@sbcglobal.net

To order books by author
visitwww.**DoNotGiveUp**.net

or call 323.964.1736

e-mail – JewelMotivates**@gmail.**com or

Jewel@DoNotGiveUp.net

Published by:
Unlock Publishing House
231 West Hampton Place
Capitol Heights, MD 20743
www.unlockpublishing.com

ISBN 13/ 978-1-60743-033-9

Printed in the United States of America January 2009

This book is dedicated to my sons John and Jason.

Yes! Your proactive step of purchasing this book will guide you closer to achieving satisfaction and gaining more practical wisdom. You have made a good choice with your time and money to cultivate your mind and habits to grow and produce prosperity, peace and positive results.

I suggest you become like a student in a classroom. Step outside of your self to study "you." In order to experience progress and success, know that, adversity, distractions, disappointments and problems to be solved, are part of the journey. Leaders and top performers in any given field are paid for solving problems and achieving results. The intent to this book is to assist you in solving problems and achieving results. The bookends for success are "starting" and finishing."

Now as a student studying the subject called "you", I want to suggest the following steps. Think about that project, business, goal or task you want to complete. This is the learning process…

1) Observe
2) Act
3) Evaluate
4) Readjust
5) Go back to step 2 and take more action.

The more you are able to honestly observe your patterns of thinking, speaking, coping, reacting, feeling and doing, the more you will be able adjust and re-calibrate. Observing the truth about your limiting behavior sets you free to experience more success.

As a speaker/teacher, the hardest message for my audiences to hear are about their eating habits, spending habits, relationship choices and fear-based thinking.
People become attached to their own expectations and habits. To change and improve, in their minds, makes them feel afraid, ashamed, embarrassed or too prideful to observe, evaluate and readjust. They are attached, tied and bond to old familiar patterns and expectations.

When your expectations in a relationship, career, friendship, parenting, school, interview or any pursuit of a goal are not met, your happiness is affected. People and life are not predictable. For most people their happiness is based on their ability to cope with change, fear and stress. One's happiness and joy are often hinged on their expectations. If expectations are not met and instead one experiences disappointment, many people lose their joy, faith and happiness. As humans we have attachments and expectations. We grow to expect something to "happen" in a certain way and at a certain time. We have expectations from others and from ourselves.

6

The word "*happ*iness" is rooted in the word "happening." If the right experiences are not *happening* most people do not feel happy. Life is not always fair, convenient or logical. Favor is not always fair.

To let go and accept what is happening in your life takes courage, faith, flexibility and even a sense of humor. When change happens like; cancer, a car accident, unemployment, loss of a loved one, allowing others to help you when you are ill grieving or aging... you will either become angry, resentful and resistant or you will adapt. As you adapt you begin to learn to let go of ego, vanity and fear. Adapting makes room for compassion, humility and a spirit of cooperation and trust.

For most of us, the word surrender brings up negative thoughts. Society teaches us that quitters never win and winners never quit. Surrender is the last thing we want to do.

To surrender to circumstances that are out of your control does not mean you are weak or losing control. To let go and say, "*it is, what it is*" does not means you are waving the white flag and giving up. To surrender to the flow of life brings about peace and opens the door to other possibilities that your resistance and anger are blocking.

Spiritually letting go is empowering. It is about choosing a way of life that embraces acceptance, joy and faith. Shift happens! I realize it can be a struggle to feel stabilized in your life when every thing is shifting and shaking and life keeps giving you unexpected surprises. Surrender is about ending the struggle in your life and beginning your journey on a path of trusting the Lord and law of life called change. It's about adapting, spiritual maturing, gratitude, maintaining your health and peace and using your creativity, imagination to adapt.

Spiritual surrender is admitting that you are not in control. A time of "shifting", loss and transition is the time to grow through the wilderness of the unknown until you reach a new ground of stabilization (your promise land). It's getting your self out of the way and trusting God's power and grace to guide you. Spiritual surrender frees you from fear and anger and grants you peace.

To honestly observe your self takes courage and love. As you honestly observe your habits with time, temper, tests of your faith, tribulations and temptation, do you see how you often you choose to ignore, deny or rationalize your behavior? Can you begin to see how you may give your power and peace away when your expectations are not met? Are you so attached to the outcome and results your ego desires that you cannot let go and let God?

Real change in your attitude, actions, diet, time management, faith, finances and relationships are not easy but they are definitely possible.

Perseverance and patience are needed to achieve results with your; weight loss, becoming debt free, becoming clean and sober, finishing your book, graduating from college, building your business/ministry, healing your heart from grief, loss, divorce or disappointment.

I have always been inspired by the many stories I learn about perseverance. One inspirational story I share as a keynote speaker for conferences is about Walt Disney. I live near Disneyland, but I have grown out of my childhood fascination and excitement about going to Disneyland. However, Walt Disney's perseverance is something that fuels my determination to keep the main thing...the MAIN THING! Disney's request for a business loan was rejected by 301 banks before he finally got approved. That loan built the famous Disneyland in California and the rest of his expansion worldwide is history.

E very January for over 20 years I teach a New Year seminar with a football theme. It is called SUPER GOAL SATURDAY. I glean a lot of practical wisdom from football coaches who empower their team to win with perseverance, skills, practice, focus and determination. It's the same set of attitudes you and I need to win in the game of life. Green Bay Packers Coach Vince Lombardi stated, "The difference between a successful person and others is not lack of strength, not a lack of knowledge, but a lack of determination."

When you are focused and determined to be an overcomer and make your touch down in life, it's because you kept the main thing...the MAIN THING! Observe leaders and top performers around you. You will observe that they did not give up. Many examples of determined souls are all around you...athletes, cancer survivors, college graduates, single parents, widowers, victims of disasters like earthquakes, floods, hurricanes and fires. I agree with Peter Lowe's quotation..."The most common trait I have found in all successful people is that they have conquered the temptation to give up."

It has always been a passion of mine to study people who overcame obstacles with their creativity, vision, faith, determination and perseverance. One example is about the aircraft industry. The Wright Brothers did not have the vision to see how airplanes could be used commercially or for the military. However, William Boeing was a visionary and saw potential outside the box the commercial value of airplanes. Boeing did not even know how to fly an airplane. He lived in Seattle, Washington but the aeronautic research was taking place on the East Coast. To fulfill his engineering vision for the future of airplanes, Boeing had to overcome the obstacles of distance and safety. Boeing financed construction of a wind tunnel at a local university to attract the engineers he needed. In 1917 the American military was preparing for World War I and needed airplanes. The problem was the Navy was testing new planes in Florida, too far to fly the little planes. So Boeing figured out how to dismantle the planes, box them up like pizzas, and ship them across the country.

For years he continued research and development on the planes while also producing boats and furniture. With the three increasing need for mail delivery, increased passenger travel and Charles Lindbergh's New York to Paris flight creating a real boom and excitement about air travel, Boeing's creativity and consistency positioned him to dominate the industry. He kept the main thing...the

MAIN THING in spite of challenges and obstacles. Many people become overwhelmed with life's demands and changes. Some people get distracted from their goal and purpose.

I use the metaphor of the GPS in our cars which gives us the map and guidance to reach a destination. In life, some times we are lost or trying to reach a new destination of success, peace and purpose. As a mentor and 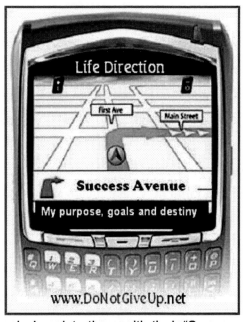 personal success coach, I assist others with their "Success GPS" system. (**G**oals, **P**urpose and **S**piritual Faith). My goal is to help them observe, evaluate and readjust their path to success.

- o What is your goal (destination)?
- o Do you see any potential road blocks?
- o Are you accountable to any one to help you stay on your path? Who are your co-passengers?

o   Are you willing to make u-turns, slow down or
    speed up?
o   Are your prepared to cope with detours, delays or
    bad weather?
o   Is your body in good health? When was your last
    tune up?
o   What type of fuel are you using (nutrition)?
o   Have you started and stopped before on this path
    because you were discouraged or lonely?
o   There is no straight line to success. Are you able
    to adapt and walk the fine line of flexibility and
    consistency? Life is like playing chess. With each
    move you take, the board changes.   The map of
    your life will change because of relationships,
    health,   age,   conflict,   stress,   uncontrollable
    circumstances, wrong turns, detours, etc.
o   Are you spiritually, financially, emotionally and
    mentally prepared for the journey?
o   Are you prepared to cope with any adversity or
    changes? There is an old wise saying, "You can
    claim to be surprised once, after that, you're just
    unprepared."

I offer on my web site a CD message "Preparation
Before Elevation".   Proper planning and prior
preparation is so critical to help you achieve results.
When I think about weddings, conferences, church

service, a football game or even my keynote presentations, it's the prior preparation that takes longer than the actual event. If you pay attention to the details, planning and the preparation, these habits give you the sustaining power to stick with your goal. General Douglas MacArthur said, "Preparedness is the key to success and victory. The more you sweat in peace, the less you bleed in war."

T ime is a gift not to be wasted. With every new birthday and every missed opportunity, I learn to appreciate and respect time more than ever before. With so many demands of my time and a desire to be effective, efficient and a woman of excellence, I don't see time has a cruel task master, but a gift from God. With each passing day remembering the passing of loved ones, I honor and appreciate the gift of life, health and time. With so many tasks to accomplish and new ideas constantly stirring in my mind, I must respect time and use it wisely to act with impact.

Time can be lost and **squandered** away on trivial and unproductive activities. Precious time can be lost because of sleep, depression, distractions, procrastination and fear. Time can be **scattered** in many directions on too many different projects yielding little results. Time can be **spent** on productive, creative, critical and goal achieving tasks.

Time can be **savored** by learning to slow down, recharge, breathe and enjoy each precious breath and moment. When we savor time, we experience gratitude, beauty and a healthy heart.   Time is priceless.   Ralph Waldo Emerson stated, "Guard well your spare moments. They are like uncut diamonds. Discard them and their value will never be known. Improve them and they will become the brightest gems in a useful life."

Being a workaholic is not healthy and likewise, being lazy and scattered is not productive.

Build up your inner integrity to keep promises to yourself about your goals and critical tasks. As you grow to respect and depend on yourself to follow through on a task or promise, you will see that your integrity with others will also be boosted. Success and happiness are rooted in good relationships.   Author Byrd Baggett defines integrity as "Doing **what** you said you would do, **when** you said you would do it and **how** you said you would do it."

To be above average, one must act with impact. Rolf Smith, the author of **The 7 Levels of Change** offers seven kinds of change to be effective in life…

1) Effectiveness – doing the right things

2) Efficiency – doing the right things right

3) Improving – doing things better

4) Cutting – doing away with things

5) Adapting – doing things other people are doing

6) Different – doing things no one else is doing

7) Impossible – doing things that can't be done

The more you are able to observe your habits, evaluate, adjust and take necessary action, the more success you will experience. Remember the importance of proper preparation, deal with distractions, focus and concentrate on your task at hand and surround yourself with the right people can influence you in a positive way.

. Unhappy and unsuccessful people focus on surviving.

. Average people focus on their thinking on maintenance

. Successful people focus their thinking on progress.

This book is presented in a way that allows for quick review. You can open any page in the future and receive a jumpstart. Be reminded that even though "shift happens" in your life...you have a choice to react in a negative, stressful and counterproductive manner or you can learn how to say *"What's my next step? ... it is what it is...*

I can trust my Heavenly Father to guide and provide for me...I can do this...I am well able... I am a conqueror...I am a winner ...I am focused on solutions... I walk by faith and not by sight... I trust myself to do the right thing...I am flexible, capable and organized to adapt and keeping pressing on...I am equipped and I won't be whipped by life's circumstances. "

B ecause **you are a creature of habit**, your habits (*knee jerk reaction to shift*) will either cause you to think the same old thoughts, take no action and behave in ways that result in loss of time, procrastination, fear, anger and stress.   Or your habits lead you to think certain thoughts and take actions that create progress, productivity and inner peace.

I congratulate you on taking a positive step in the right direction as I partner with you to point out guideposts on your road to success.   Mentoring you through my written word and CDs can assist in clearing your mind of sabotaging thoughts like fear, doubt, stress and

17

unhappiness.   Your mind will be encouraged and empowered to grow.

Some ideas will seem simplistic. Some ideas may seem too challenging and take you out of your comfort zone. Some ideas you already know, but need the reinforcement to continue growing and achieving the life you desire. Open your mind to be teachable. Commit to a goal. Make a commitment to upgrade the quality of your thinking and life.   Always remember this…your ego/subconscious mind **does not** like new thoughts introduced. It guards against "identity thief." What has been your identity? --- the loser, fat, stupid, poor, unattractive, the trouble maker, the superwoman, the fixer, the baby in the family, the controller, the survivor?

Would you like to train your brain to; be more effective, think big, believe in yourself, forgive and let go of the past , be fearless, be move loving and stop sabotaging behavior?

Would you like to experience confidence, faith, wealth, weight loss, adventure, new love, inner peace, a healing in your family, a healthier lifestyle, a meaningful career, promotion on your job, a successful interview, increase in business sales, larger circle of true friends, trust and intimacy, a purpose driven life, inner strength to endure shift and storms, a deeper faith, a rich spiritual life and salvation from a broken past?

If your answer is "yes" to a new identity... the repetition and review is a necessary habit that knocks on the door of your ego/ subconscious mind which guards and protects your old mental tapes.

The old tapes like "poor me" are in the subconscious mind. That is why it is difficult for some people to believe they can be a millionaire, happy, healthy, in a loving relationship, have a better career, be clean and sober and experience the grace, favor and blessings of God. Their thoughts of unworthiness are in the "identity file."

Review and repetition of inspirational and educational materials will help you create a new identity of worthiness, capability and prosperity. New habits, thoughts and your better self will rise and the old self dies.

When you are sick and tired of being sick, tired, broke, addicted, lost, lonely, angry, depressed and stressed and when **you are willing to dedicate** your time and efforts to growth --- you will need constant review and repetition.

If you knock on some one's door one time and you leave because no one answered the door, that doesn't mean no one was there. Maybe they didn't want to let you in. I have certainly done that before. I heard the knock on my door, but I didn't want a stranger to enter...so I didn't open the door.

19

Reading this book or any inspirational material one time is a **not** enough. Your ego/subconscious mind needs *constant knocking on the door* before it opens to receive new strange thoughts. Your ego protects your false identity of being *a loser, the addict, the shy one, the martyr, a failure, struggling poor, a victim, fat and ugly, stupid, the workaholic, superwoman, the sick one, the enforcer, the rescuer, the wild child, the saint, the perfectionist, passive or superior to others, etc.*

The enemy to your success and happiness is counting on you to give up and act like a punk, a cry baby, weak, depressed, distracted, tempted, stubborn, prideful, lazy, unfocused, helpless, ignorant, jealous, scared, angry and act like a victim.

God's power is within you waiting for you to make a choice fueled by desperation or inspiration. There is a secret power of strength, love, courage, wisdom, joy, abundance, creativity, imagination, generosity, compassion and success yet unborn. Open your mind, heart and soul.

Each time you review this message you are making an impression on your subconscious mind that you are serious about making positive changes in your life.

I highly suggest you create the habit of having a daily list of things-to-do which acts as your **compass** giving you direction. Indicate on your list which tasks are critical, necessary or low priority. Learn to delegate (not dump) and ask for help. Frequently refer to your **clock** and **calendar** to keep your self organized and punctual.

Pray to develop the wisdom, discernment, focus, resources and discipline and concentration to finish what you start. What ever direction your attention goes, so does your energy and results. Where ever your attention flows, the energy and favor of God follows. When you decide, God provides. People and circumstances begin to line up with your clear intention, attention and decisions.

Every day you are faced with decisions to make --- big and small. In fact, the quality of your life depends on your ability to make good decisions. Your degree of happiness or misery is based on your decisions. Your health and wealth grows or diminishes based on your ability to make wise decisions.

There are 3 types of decisions -- 1) say "**yes**" to do it, 2) say "**no**" against an action, 3) **avoid** making a decision, which is a decision of inaction.

I believe most people get off track with their goals and lose enthusiasm because of the following reasons:

21

1. Lack **clarity**. Not specific and sure about their intentions. Doubt and fear hold them back.

2. Poor past **choices** with time, money, talent or relationships have them in a stronghold of pain and shame.

3. **Complacency** - a feeling of quiet pleasure or security, unaware of some potential danger. Self-satisfaction or smug satisfaction with an existing situation, condition, etc.

4. Life **circumstances** (i.e. divorce, layoff, health, family issues, accident, grief, etc.) have interrupted their dreams and plans.

5. Lack self-**control** with time, money, emotions and other **compulsive** bad habits.

6. Being a **creature of habit**, the sabotaging habit of; procrastination, **clutter**, fear and starting and stopping a project and poor **concentration** has deferred their success and sense of satisfaction.

7. **Caregivers** tend to make their life and goals less of a priority and put off tasks to take care of others.

8. Too **concerned** about what other people think. Fear of criticism, fear of failure or fear of success.

My personal le$$ons of procrastination in the past have resulted in my loss of sleep, money, time and important papers.

I'm excited that I can share my pearls of wisdom with you in these pages. It's never too late to learn. I'm glad you are teachable and ready to change the direction of your life. **Preparation** is always necessary before **elevation**. Self-honesty is your staring point.

- ✓ Why did you choose to read this material now?
- ✓ What do you want to accomplish?
- ✓ What do you think is holding you back?
- ✓ What sabotaging behavior patterns are you willing to break?
- ✓ Have you allowed unfortunate circumstances to rob you of your enthusiasm, determination, faith and self-esteem?
- ✓ What is your point of pain?
- ✓ What is your passion?
- ✓ Have you been scattering your attention and time?
- ✓ What strong**holds, habits, hurts or hang ups** are keeping you from fully realizing your potential for growth, success and happiness?

Y ou can experience success and satisfaction by **directing your attention on your intention**. As you change how you think, you will change the results you see in your life.

In the beginning you may not see results, but the more you apply what you learn, you will see the success principles actually working in your life because of your consistency.

Blessings and opportunities are every where. You will begin to attract your definition of success and happiness the more you understand that you reap what you sow.

What thoughts are you sowing? **If** those seeds are nurtured with consistent action, faith, belief, expectation and feelings, your thoughts eventually grow up and show up in your life.

Energy flows to the direction of your sustained focused of negative or positive attention. In other words, **faith and fear are both expecting something to happen.** God's supernatural power flows to your sustained faith focus. And like wise, energy flows to your sustained feelings of fear – which is call self-fulfilling prophesy. You tend to get what you expect.

Because I am a visual learner, I created the following illustration. This helps me to see and hopefully show others about the flow of energy. This is my "faith funnel."

Sustained Focus Attention

Thoughts   Feelings

Actions   Time

Images

Words

Energy

Spiritual Power

Results

Think on this principle. See how important it is to **keep** your main goal-desire-intention-wish sustained with your thoughts, feelings, actions, images and words. Over time, keeping the main thing…the MAIN THING accelerates God's energy to flow towards your laser beam targeted pre-determined results you focus on.

Sometimes I split my computer screen and have several programs going at once. Soon I notice my computer responds slower. Do you "split focus" your life like a Windows Program? The more you multi-task, scatter your energy, say "yes' to many demands and focus on trivial activities, you lose ground. If you have too many "funnels", the flow of energy and effectiveness becomes weakened. Results come from the ability to concentrate.

The negative and toxic emotions of anger, doubt, fear, guilt, resentment, shame, unhappiness and stress tend to attract unpleasant and costly results.

Fear

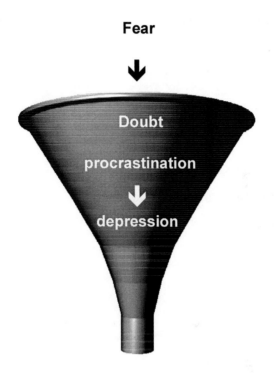

UNPLEASANT RESULTS

Become mindful of what you are concentrating on. Work every day to **become more aware** of your emotional triggers, feelings, thoughts and habits that block your joy, progress and positive actions. Once you acknowledge your sabotaging behavior, you can, with time, break them and create more positive patterns of behavior.

My life is far from perfect. However, I discovered I am able to cope better with the ups and downs of life because I feel I'm living in my true purpose and passion. What a blessing! I had a vision for my speaking career. I was not using my talents and gifts in Human Resources at Hughes Aircraft.

I was determined to turn my passion of speaking and teaching into a profitable profession.

I picked up spiritual assignment in the late 80's to be a public speaker and never looked back. For over 20 years I've had a j-o-y and not a j-o-b. My focus wasn't just about making money, but a quest for meaning and making a difference in the lives of other people. I find great joy in serving you *food for your soul* as one of your teachers and guideposts to discover your purpose and success.

Harold Kushner author of **When Bad Things Happen to Good People** says, *"Our souls are not hungry for fame, comfort, wealth or power. Our souls are hungry for meaning, for the sense that we have figured out how to live so that our lives matter, so that the world will at least be a little bit different for our having passed through it."*
Composer Gian Carlo Menotti believes, "Hell begins on that day when God grants us a clear vision of all that we

might have achieved, of all the gifts we wasted, of all that we might have done **but** we **did not do**."

There is a price you pay for success. There is price to pay when you don't follow your dreams and use your talents.

Adding meaning to your life does not always mean quitting or changing your job. How do you use your time and talents beyond your work time? Who do you mentor?

How are you helping your community locally or globally? What assets are you sitting on? What activity gives you joy?

Reading this message often will help you to let go of pain, doubt and procrastination. Take a deep breath and begin to pursue your passion today. It's never too late to start.

Who **adds** to your life? They will expand your possibilities. Who **drains** you? They can steal your joy, peace, health and success. How do you spend your **time**? Time is your resource. There are no ordinary moments. Every day is a gift of life.

 **What** is **your intention** (i. e. goal, desire, aim, purpose, course of action, plan, focus, etc.)**?**

What are you clearly purposing in your mind that needs to happen in order for you to experience satisfaction, achievement, fulfillment, joy and completion of your "written down" goals?

Who and **what** gets your **attention?**

The right people in your life can add the right energy, influence, resources, inspiration and encouragement you need.

Giving your attention, time, energy and power away to the wrong people is so defeating. Develop emotional and time boundaries to keep your distance from the negative pull of others who do not honor, respect or align with your values and vision.

Are the people and activities that absorb your time gett..
you **further** or **closer** to the realization and completion of
your pre-determined and clear goals?

Once you learn to be CLEAR about your **intention**, direct
your **attention** and actions towards that **direction.**

Once you harness the **power of focused concentration**
and **discipline,** you will begin to **achieve incredible
success, a sense of satisfaction and self-esteem.**

Your discipline is developed as you learn **to do what
you have to do now** ... so you can **enjoy in the future
what you really want to do, be or have.**

Discipline is the **ability to say "no"** to those **distractions
and temptations. You are in essence saying "yes" to
your goal.**

hts, clutter and double-minded thinking can

s, confusion and a sense of failure.

esponsibility, confrontation, criticism
...g a people pleaser will certainly stop you
..om achieving your goal.

Once you **resolve** in your mind **"what" is the main thing** you want to accomplish today, this week, this month, this year, in your life time... then the main thing... **is to keep** the MAIN thing...**the MAIN THING!**

A re you in a dry place where nothing is growing in your life and everyday is full of stress and strife?

Hold on, breathe, and remember every day

God is still worthy to be praised. Read my book "You Are Too Blessed to Be Stressed."

When you've given all you got

and every door seems to close

and all you hear is "no"

when a relationship bitterly ends

or death takes a family member or friend

when dreams and plans don't come true

and the rent is way past due

When your business sales are low

or your weight loss seems slow

when the child support doesn't come in the mail

or the class assignment you fail

when after the interview you don't hear "hired"

or your children make you feel worried and tired

when the one you love won't call back ---

these are the times the enemy seems to attack.

You may feel weak, stressed and confused.

Give your broken pieces to God and you won't lose.

It may be dark and you don't feel strong right now.

You may not see when, why, who or how.

Stay in God's light and you will be guided in what to

do. Just put on your faith walking shoes.

Don't compromise with the devil and make a deal.

Your finances, health and heart will heal. I know it may feel scary, lonely and hard just remember God has brought you this far.

Don't give up during this challenging test.
Your change will come, you will soon hear "yes"
Yes, it would be great to have the help and support
from family and friends so dear
but when they are **not** near,
fight to keep away the depression and fear.
Take your spiritual weapons off the shelf.
and learn how to encourage yourself.

.

Train your brain for success.

Don't be tired…get inspired !

Get equipped so you can't be whipped by stress.

Y ou must be focused and yet know how to adapt to change and unexpected circumstances.

SHIFT happens! Changes will happen without your permission. In spite of a good plan and good intentions, you will need to know how to adjust and adapt and regroup.

After a setback, it's easier to get back on track with your goals when your intentions (goals, desire, plan) are written down, clear, reinforced, measurable and **re-visited often**.

Have you ever experienced the excitement and enthusiasm about a new goal? You start off with good intentions and consistency and then you hit a wall. That has happened to me many times, especially when it comes to being consistent with physical exercise. I can be consistent for two months going to the gym 3 - 4 times a week. And then it either becomes boring or I allow excuses and distractions to break my momentum. It becomes a chore to get my behind out of the house and attend my step, yoga and aerobics classes.

MAIN THING goal" is to have energy, good
keep my weight down. I've had to learn how
and push myself to go beyond my excuses
and loss of enthusiasm. I can't afford to be distracted by
other minor tasks and the TV.

I began to hear the voice in my head reminding me
that if I stopped, it would be difficult to begin again.
If I stopped, I would feel bad about myself because
I broke a promise to myself. If I stopped, I wouldn't
achieve my weight loss goal.

I go to the gym and YES!...I overcome my *lethargic –
I don't wanna go - I don't see any results - I'll go
tomorrow - procrastinating* attitude.

Getting up and getting it done is not about how I feel,
it's about my discipline, commitment and consistency.
Keeping the main thing, the MAIN THING helps me to
gain some self-esteem points also because I am keeping
my promises. This strengthens integrity and resolve.

B e reminded today that whatever MAIN THING GOAL you have, it will require you to be **self**-motivated.

Notice if you feel yourself slowing down, distracted, losing faith and enthusiasm. Keep your eye on your goal and **not** your feelings. Your feelings will fool, criticize and discourage you.

Today you may **not** "feel" like doing your paper work, going to the gym, making more customer calls, showing up for work, cleaning up your clutter, preparing your taxes, writing your business plan, saving money, going on more job interviews or studying to graduate.

All successful relationships are built on **trust**. First you must learn to trust yourself. Begin to trust yourself to: do the right thing, keep your promises, speak up for yourself and protect and nurture your dreams and talents.

The Bible teaches us that our spirit and our flesh will war against each other in this life. Our flesh wants immediate self-gratification at all costs and will stop at nothing to try and get it. Our spirit knows that some of our fleshly desires are not right for us and as a result, there will be a tug of war between the two - and sometimes it will be a major tug of war. And the only thing that will be able to curb and control some of the desires of our flesh is the quality of self-control.

Self-control is the ability to regulate **your thinking** and conduct by principle and sound judgment, rather than by impulse, desire, or social custom. Biblically, self-discipline may be summarized in one word: **obedience.** To exercise self-discipline is to avoid evil and harm by staying within the bounds of God's law.

PROBLEM	EXCUSE - Justification
Overweight	"I don't have time to eat right!"
	"Water has no taste or sugar."
Procrastination	"I can only do so much in a day! I can always do it tomorrow."
Always in debt	"They don't pay me enough!"
	"I work hard and deserve to shop."
Stressed out	"I never have time to relax!"
Work performance	"If they paid me more – I'd do more!"
Smoking	"I need it for stress relief! I can quit anytime."

PROBLEM	EXCUSE - Justification
Drinking/Drugs	"One drink never hurt anybody!" "I can quit anytime."
Poor nutrition	"I don't have time to prepare a meal." "Fast food is quicker."
No daily exercise	"I just can't find the time! Exercise messes up my hair."
Anger- Temper	"They had it coming to them!"
Depression	"Nothing ever goes right for me!" "I can't help myself."
Poor appearance	"It's the newest fashion!" "Nobody cares what I look like."
Divorce	"We just couldn't work it out!"
Lack of Self-discipline	"I have enough things to worry about! I deserve to have what I want **now**."
Tardiness	"I have so much to do. No one will help me. I can't help it."
Clutter/Disorder	"I might need this later. I don't have time to clean up."

Some days you will have energy and enthusiasm and sometimes your "get up and go" --- will *get up and go!* Be reminded now that you must discipline and motivate yourself to overcome the temptation to stop, sleep, socialize and avoid the task at hand. Former NBA player Jerry West said, "*You can't get much done in life if you only work on the days you feel good.*"

The quality of your life and reaching success in your life depends on your ability to motivate yourself **beyond** how you feel. You can develop self-control by becoming aware of your urges. Self-control acts as a **filter** against the **powerful influence of advertising, accessibility, and your own destructive personal habits**.

We live in a society where it is hard NOT to be fat, lazy, unhealthy, drugged up, bankrupt, depressed, or emotionally unstable. This society has created so many conveniences, trends, wants, and erratic behaviors through advertising and mass media, that **we are brainwashed to crave things**. When you have the ability to concentrate, focus on your goals, and consistently stay with your priorities by keeping the main thing...THE MAIN THING, you will increase your chances for success and the blessings of God.

Suggested reading ☛ www.DoNotGiveUp.net/**stressless**.htm

Who could you become? What could you experience? What could you have if you really read, studied, focused, saved, prayed, networked, asked for help, got out of your comfort zone, used your time wisely, served others and gave your all?

Procrastination is a thief. Things are not going to change unless you change. Life is fragile, wonderful, short and subject to change. Guard your wealth, health and significant relationships both personal and professional. Learn to serve others and realize that confidence, integrity and service to others are a shortcut to increase success.

Discipline, patience, prayer, planning, perseverance and proactive activity will pay off. To make a resolution in your mind means you are determined and have cleared away the doubt. To resolve an intention in your life means it is

settled, decided, firm

and **followed up with**

some form of **action.**

7 things that will block your growth are....

1. lack of information, skills, education

2. fear, worry, over caution, procrastination

3. doubt, low self-esteem, indecision, double minded

4. lack of planning, concentration and focused action

5. pessimistic, complaining

6. lack of positive influences and relationships

7. indifference, depression, scattered thinking

Grow out of your comfort zone.

Take a leap of faith and action.

Letting go of old sabotaging habits opens you up to infinite possibilities. You can have more peace of mind, success and a sense of accomplishment.

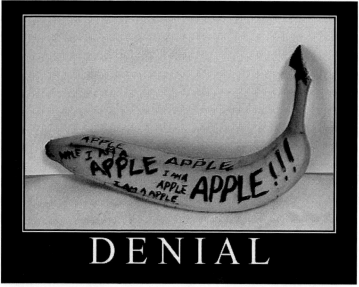

DENIAL

Denial in any form is costly and will cause you to procrastinate. Be willing to admit and work on the deficiencies in your character, habits, skills and lifestyle.

Denial about your health issues won't make the problems or weight go away. Get on the scale. Seek medical help.

Not opening your bills or not answering the phone won't make the bill collectors go away.

You cannot fix want you don't face. You can change what you don't confront with courage.

Your life can't change unless you change your thinking.

If you feel stuck on your path and need to be rescued, become what I call a **Triple AAA thinker**.

Acknowledge where you are in truth without denial, anger or blame.

Analyze your options and next step. Break goals down into small manageable steps.

Now take progressive **A**CTION steps.

That's AAA thinking!

Make a list of the things you can change. Start there with some action and a plan. You only lose time and energy if you continue to whine, wait, worry, weep and wish things were better. Instead of telling God about your big problems, tell your problems that you have a big God. Advance by associating with achievers.

Put yourself in a blessing position by associating with people on-the-grow. Fly with eagles. Talk with teachers. Walk with winners. Climb with champions. Study successful people. Their success, experience and insights are contagious. Seek spiritual guidance.

Feeling stuck, fearful, prideful, depressed and unworthy is **dis**empowering. Being double-minded, wishy-washy and uncertain blocks yours growth. Negative emotions are like a block wall. This wall of emotions blocks all the positive opportunities and blessings.

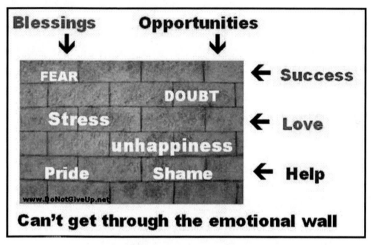

You become empowered as you demonstrate the courage to make a decision and follow through with action

Are you ready and willing to tear down any block walls that hinder your growth?

It takes **repetition** *(i.e. constant hammering to chip away blockages)* to remove old tapes in your head. One time is not enough to tear down your emotional walls of resistance and fear.

What was important to you some time ago may not be a priority in your life now. Write your own personal mission statement for success. This will be **your compass** when you get lost, distracted or discouraged.

Isolation can breed an environment of depression and incompletion of goals. **Be accountable** to a friend, family member, mentor, success coach or support circle to help you achieve your goals for life enrichment.

Strengthening your faith, self-esteem and self-determination will help you endure the tough times, enjoy your life and excel in your goals.

In the midst of a challenge, I often stop and watch a comedy show or call up a good friend to enjoy some laughs which puts everything back into perspective. Having a sense of humor when life doesn't make any sense is good medicine for the weary and wounded soul. Take time for laughter and lighten up.

Pray, plan, prepare, pursue passionately, persist and believe that you are worthy and capable of achieving your definition of prosperous living.

Real estate giant, wealth coach and author Robert Kiyosaki states he focuses on his real estate acquisitions by remembering this acronym.

F – follow
O – on
C – course
U – until
S – successful

Don't quit because you're alone.

Don't quit because it's tough.

Don't quit because you're out of your comfort zone.

Don't quit because you're mad.

Don't quit because you're sad.

Don't quit because no one seems to help or care.

Don't quit because it's taking so long.

Don't quit because you see no reward.

Don't quit because you think it's too late.

Don't quit...stick with it.

Speak victory into your life.

Speak success into your life.

Speak determination into your life.

Speak love into your life.

Speak strength and courage into your life.

Direct your action and attention on your intention.

D-O I-T N-O-W.

Here is an easy way to remember this rule...

D = Divide and conquer what you have to do. Break big tasks into smaller pieces and give each piece a realistic deadline.

O = Organize your materials. Plan how you will tackle the job.

I = Ignore interruptions. Come in early or stay after hours to assure needed quiet time to complete important projects.

T = Take the time to learn how to do certain essential things yourself instead of always having to wait for a assistant, consultant or some other helper to do it for you.

N = Now, don't procrastinate. Put the task you have been dreading and avoiding the most at the top of your to-do list.

O = Opportunity is knocking. Take advantage of opportunities. Follow through, ask, seek and knock.

W = Watch out for time gobblers such as the Internet, e-mail, watching TV, talking on the phone. But do make time to have lunch, exercise and take vacations to recharge your batteries and reconnect with your family and friends.

How can I pay more attention to my intention?

⊙ What is your aim?

⊙ A clear mind and your health are needed. Strengthen your immune system and keep your energy up with proper rest, nutritious food, water and exercise.

⊙ Write down your vision. What is your intention? What do you want to achieve?

⊙ Use and keep your calendar, clock and compass (goal direction) in view to keep you on track with time and deadlines.

⊙ Brainshare - delegate and distribute tasks. Enlist the talents, gifts, ideas and help from others; share in responsibilities and resources.

⊙ Learn how to say "no" to distractions, invitations and requests for your time, money and energy.
Prepare for your project and environment by having the tools and resources ready so you can focus. Clear up your working and living environment. Get rid of the clutter in your working and living space.

⊙ Unplug from the world. Plan and honor uninterrupted scheduled time with no phones, e-mails, children, TV, games, unscheduled appointments, etc.

⊙ Keep your faith strong. Feeding your spirit on the word of God will give you the strength, comfort, wisdom, faith and guidance you'll need to sustain you through the difficult changes of life.

A void burnout being a multi-tasker, juggling too many ideas, projects and demands. Decide and act on your priorities first. If you are the "fixer" and "go to person" in the family and you allow everyone to dump on you, your priorities, sanity, self-esteem and progress will suffer. Learn how to say "no" to the demands, guilt and unrealistic requests from others.

Let go of the other tasks or delegate them to others. Tap into your left brain skills to strategize, create a plan and order. A left brain style of achieving a task enhances your ability to be more organized, precise, detail-oriented, sequential and focused.

Left Brain Thinkers

You are a creature of habit. If you tend to be more **left brain** dominant in approaching a task, you may seek perfection. You may *over think* the process and suffer from paralysis of analysis. You may need too many guarantees to avoid mistakes and feeling embarrassed. You may be isolated and lack people skills. You are less likely to achieve a goal because of rigid thinking and the inability to cope with changes and unpredictable circumstances. You probably have a plan **but lack faith, imagination and strong people skills to get started.**

Typical attributes of a "left brain" thinker are:

. analytical, gathers facts

. rational

. organized and needs structure and system

. punctual

. measures precisely

. reliable, maintains consistency

. direct, realistic, critical

. plays it safe, rigid

. reads the fine print

. cautious, does not like deviation or surprises

. good with numbers, stats, keeps good financial records

. a loner, minimal low social skills

Right Brain Thinkers

If you are **right brain** dominant, your goals and tasks may not be clear. You may have a lot of great ideas, but lack planning skills to get started. You may be easily distracted. You may be a dreamer instead of a doer.

You are more likely to stop and start and deviate from instructions and a plan of action. It is difficult to keep the main thing, the main thing if you are scattered, unclear or impulsive.

Typical attributes of a "right brain" thinker are:

. recognizes new possibilities

. problem solving in intuitive ways

. optimistic, enthusiastic, expressive

. tolerates ambiguity

. sees the big picture

. curious, speculates

. multi-tasking

. goes with the flow

. likes surprises, takes risks

You may exhibit some or all of these attributes in your working style, relationships and goal setting. The ideal approach **to complete a task** is to **use both sides of your brain.** Maximize your potential for success by being a good planner, yet flexible. Dream and visualize your outcome and yet learn how to be strategic and time conscious.

Left brain style	Right brain style
Analytical	Creative, Dreamer
Logical	Visual
Punctual	Go with flow
Repetitive	Empathetic
Math	Abstract
Details	Sees bigger picture
Literal	Explorer
Sequential	Musical
Predictable	Spontaneous
Paperwork oriented	People oriented
Planner	In the moment
Needs order	Easily bored
Strategist/Planner	Experimental
Stressed/irritable	Flexible
Perfectionist	Impulsive
Acts on facts	Acts by faith
Resists change	Enjoys change
Has a system	Random

The ideal way to cope and to achieve success is to engage both sides of your brain. Become aware of your habits and personality type.

If you are dominantly left brain in your approach to tasks, you will tend to get stuck in the "thinking stage" to the point that you never get started.

If you are dominantly right brain in your approach to a task, you could get stuck in the "dreaming" stage to the point that you never get in the "doing" mode.

Left brain logic, planning and details for some of your tasks and life circumstances will be your asset. In other situations your right brain faith, imagination and people skills will serve you well.

Both domains of your brain can be a liability or an asset when you are problem solving and pursuing a goal.

Become aware of your pattern and tendencies so you can create balance. Commit to honest assessment of your style of thinking so you can make appropriate adjustments.

 It's been said that the only constant in our world today is change. There may be imposed changes in your life that are mind blowing and life altering (i.e. *death of loved one, divorce, violence, hurricane, war/combat experiences, negative health diagnosis).*

Fear and pessimism can become a self-fulfilling prophesy. If you have already said you are defeated or you cannot improve, you will no longer even try, which makes it more likely your circumstances will stay the way they are or get worse

Faith and optimism will cause you to react to setbacks with the expectation of results and relief because of your faith, personal power and efforts. You see your difficulties as temporary setbacks --- isolated to particular circumstances and you feel you can overcome them with effort, faith and time.

Fear and pessimism are emotional "quick sand". The person who lives with fear reacts to setbacks with an attitude of helplessness, unworthiness and spiritual bankruptcy. Living with fear, doubt and pessimism causes one to perceive their difficulties and bad events will last a long time. This person feels like a victim blaming others.

Or they feel inadequate and feel everything is their fault thus leading to a life of shame. This person does not expect change or relief.

Faith and fear are **both expecting** something to happen. Faith expects something good to happen. Fear expects something bad to happen. Fear is exhausting. Faith is liberating. If you can change how you think, you can change how you feel. When you change how you feel --- you change how you act.

Life can be a journey or a "trip" --- Are you going to be a whiner or a winner in life? An African proverb teaches that "it rains on everyone's roof."

When "shift" happens in your life you can either choose to feel bitter, helpless, resentful, angry and afraid. Or you can choose to yield to the circumstances out of your control and gain wisdom, compassion, spiritual insights and future coping skills. It's not always the shift situation that causes unhappiness. It's your thoughts about it. When the bad feelings come you don't have to chase, push, fight, flee, cave in or suppress them. Let them come in and go out like a swinging door. The feeling will pass.

The following points are great to use as a mind strategy to figure out your next step when "shift" happens:

1. **Assessment** – Where am I now? What can I do now? What are my options?

2. **Alignment** – Not everyone is on the same page with me with regard to time, availability, attitude, values, capabilities, willingness and faith. Who and what is lined up with my values and needs to support me through this change?

3. **Attitude** – What is my disposition? What do I really believe? Where is my faith? Do I feel confident in my problem solving skills? Do I feel like a victim? Is what I'm doing and thinking right now helping or hindering me? How can I bring peace and power back into my life?

4. **Advantage** – What can I do next to leverage myself to rise above these circumstances? What do I know? Who do I know? What tools, resources, ideas, education, contacts and experiences can I draw from?

5. Play the hand I have been dealt the best way I can with a plan of **ACTION** and follow it.

Are you going to talk about your fears or your faith? Shift happens! Assess your stress. Is what you're going through life threatening or just an inconvenience?

Is your *shift stress* critical or trivial?   Is it an emergency or exaggerated? Is your stress major or momentary? Are you optimistic or pessimistic? Will you be cranky or calm today? Are you living fearless or frustrated?

The following Hawaiian proverb inspires people to remain calm in the face of difficulty:

He po'i na kai uli, kai ko'o, 'a'ohe hina puko'a
Though the sea be deep and rough, the coral rock remains standing

Remain focused on stabilizing your life and mind. I believe prayer changes things. Let no one weaken your walk of faith and determination. Honestly face your fears minimizing anger, shame and procrastination.   Remain teachable. Establish accountability relationships to keep you encouraged and proactive. Enlist others involved to move in the same direction with unity and clear communication.   Embrace change with faith and confidence remembering how you positively coped with change in the past.

Make a list of the things you can change. Start there with some action and a plan. You only lose time and energy if you continue to whine, wait, worry, weep and wish things were better.   Instead of telling God about your big problems, tell your problems that you have a big God.

Advance by associating with achievers. Put yourself in a blessing position by associating with people on-the-grow.

Fly with eagles. Talk with teachers. Walk with winners. Climb with champions. Study successful people.

Their success, experience and insights are contagious. Seek sacred and spiritual guidance.

Worry comes from fear, and the only thing that will dissolve fear is facing the facts with faith. Fully trust in God's grace in the difficult and divine cycles of life.

"I will bless the Lord who counsels me; He gives me wisdom in the night. He tells me what to do."

~ Psalm 16:7

"I will guide you in the way of wisdom."

~ Proverb 4:11

When you become too accustomed at what you are doing – too bored or too familiar – you go through each day unaware of your habits, reactions and choices. You are in a trance. You eventually live on "auto pilot" where your habits and familiarity do all the work for you – and that is a danger zone because you fall asleep at the wheel of your life. You get hit on the blind side with problems you didn't see coming. You take the same path of least resistance and develop weak responses to the shifts, bumps, detours, bad weather and uphill shifts you need to endure.

On the road of life there will shifts in our economy, the weather, your body, your family dynamics, your career, etc.

While we accept that change is a basic law of nature, we struggle when it reshapes the familiar and breaks up the continuity in our lives. Change can bring growth or grief. Change can be minor, radical, life altering, exciting, challenging, even frightening, but it can also be managed.

Just like the seasons change, your life changes. You want to be open to the change that is coming and willing to learn the lesson it often offers.

If you have a willingness to work through the initial emotional discomfort as you move step-by-step into this new lifestyle, you'll find the confidence, commitment, determination, and belief in your own self-worth that will take you to the next level.

After change, loss, controversy and chaos, there is a cleansing and healing that takes place. What used to be insignificant is now significant. Shift wakes you up and stirs you up. Shift screams, "wake up...pay attention!"

Life isn't always fair. Only the strong survive. Life is like a jungle with eagles soaring, lions prowling, snakes crawling and birds singing. There are mountains to climb, valleys to grow out of, rivers to cross, quick sand to avoid, bridges over troubled waters, beautiful flowers and rainbows to see.

When shift happens in your life, energy and time are wasted when you wish, wait, whine and worry. No one will be more committed or concerned about the quality of your life than you. Do what you need to do to bring harmony, progress, peace of mind and stability into your life.

◆ **Prioritize** your needs, wants, desires and next step.

◆ **Realize** where you are sabotaging your growth.

◆ **Organize** your living and working space.

◆ **Visualize** the outcomes you want to experience.

◆ **Utilize** your time well. Procrastination is a thief.

◆ **Recognize** your value, worth, strengths and count your blessings.

◆ **Minimize** your shortcomings, stress, toxic relationships and resistance to change.

◆ **Maximize** your opportunities and vision.

◆ **Energize** your body with sufficient rest, healthy food, plenty of water and some form of exercise.

◆ **Innergize** your faith, self-esteem and determination.

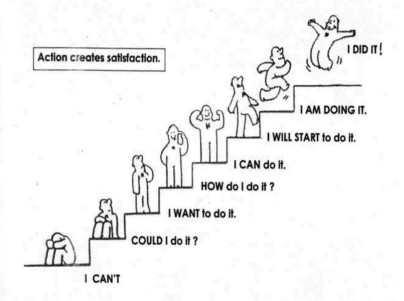

Action creates satisfaction.

I DID IT!

I AM DOING IT.

I WILL START to do it.

I CAN do it.

HOW do I do it?

I WANT to do it.

COULD I do it?

I CAN'T

B ecause we don't like to be inconvenienced or hurt, we create walls, defenses, opinions, emotional masks and addictions to protect us or numb us.   Stuff happens. It's good to practice positive thinking, pray, prepare, plan and persistently pursue your dreams and goals.   Enjoy the process of growing and achieving without becoming attached to outcomes.   Human nature seeks guarantees, safety, predictability and avoidance of pain.   Learn to adapt and accept uncertainty in life. Don't allow bad times to make you bitter. Don't allow difficult times to steal your joy, peace of mind and health. The goal is to be able to remain open to solutions, sustain your faith and accept unpleasant circumstances without shutting down and stressing out. Remind yourself every day that you can make it and you can take it.   Please do not fool yourself to think you can protect yourself from pain, stress and suffering.

www.DoNotGiveUp.net

"Life is like a box of chocolates. You never know what you're going to get." ~ Forrest Gump movie quote

In spite of any changes, suffering or stress in your life and in this world...it is a choice to rejoice. It is a daily choice to focus on your blessings as you relax into the acceptance that you cannot control other people or circumstances. Where are you on your emotional map?

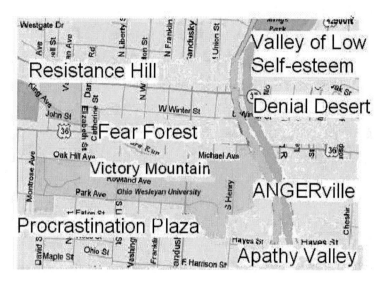

With a refreshed mind and a grateful heart you can experience a peace that surpasses all understanding.

You can learn to be comfortable with the unknown. You can stop clinging to false security and respond to changes in your life without anger, denial or familiar habits of escape or isolation.

Feelings of impatience and stress are a sign to re-evaluate your reactions to what **you cannot control** or **a wake up call** to change what you can control. Once we recognize and accept the circumstances we can't change, then we should learn to change the way we respond to them. We can choose to stay in peace **or** fall to pieces.

"The ultimate measure of a man is not where he stands in moments of comfort and convenience, but where he stands at times of challenge and controversy."

~ Dr. Martin Luther King, Jr.

The gem cannot be polished without friction, nor man perfected without trials.   ~ Chinese Proverb

There are **four styles of coping skills** described by authors by Alan J. Rowe and Richard O. Mason.

1. Analytical Style – technical, logical, careful, methodical, needs much data, likes order, enjoys problem-solving, enjoys structure, enjoys scientific study, and enjoys working alone.

2. Conceptual Style – creative and artistic, future oriented, likes to brainstorm, wants independence, uses judgment, optimistic, uses ideas vs. data, looks at the big picture, rebellious and opinionated, and committed to principles or a vision.

3. Behavioral Style – supportive of others, empathetic, wants affiliation, nurtures others, communicates easily, uses instinct, avoids stress, avoids conflict, relies on feelings instead of data, and enjoys team/group efforts.

4. Directive Style – aggressive, acts rapidly, takes charge, persuasive and/or is manipulative, uses rules, needs power/status, impatient, productive, single-minded, and enjoys individual achievements.

As you review these styles, which one best describes your coping pattern?

Analytical coping strategy – You see change as a challenging puzzle to be solved. You need plenty of time to gather information, analyze data, and draw conclusions. You will resist change if you are not given enough time to think it through.

Conceptual coping strategy – You are interested in how change fits into the big picture. You want to be involved in defining what needs to change and why. You will resist change if you feel excluded from participating in the change process.

Behavioral coping strategy – You want to know how everyone feels about the changes ahead. You work best when you know that the whole group is supportive of each other and that everyone champions the change process. If the change adversely affects someone in the group, you will perceive change as a crisis.

Directive coping strategy – You want specifics on how the change will affect you and what your own role will be during the change process. If you know the rules of the change process and the desired outcome, you will act rapidly and aggressively to achieve change goals. You resist change if the rules or anticipated results are not clearly defined.

You will experience private moments of victory without applause, points, awards, a hug or a pat on the back. But God sees you and hears you. You are growing every day in courage, action and faith.

Acknowledge your progress and walk through your valley of fear confident with the whole armor of God, the belt of truth, the shield of faith, the helmet of salvation and the sword of the spirit

What does it mean to endure?

To carry on through with faith and courage despite hardships, to make the best of a tough situation, to bear, cope with, to live through, press on, to persevere, to stick on, to suffer, to go on, to breathe, to prevail, live through, persist, pull through, ride out, press on, adapt, survive, weather the storm, withstand and "grow" to the other side of your circumstances.

Keep your eyes, ears, heart and mind open to infinite possibilities. Wherever your attention and mind goes ...your behind follows.

As you change your thoughts and habits, you will get **relief** from your stress and **results** with your goals.

Nothing you have done has been a waste of time. Every thing you have been through is a stepping stone to your next level.

Don't let boredom, depression, fear or procrastination steal your joy or success.

You may think you should have achieved more by now in this stage of your life. Are you at the crossroads needing to make a decision and asking... *where do I go from here?*

Are you in a strange and unfamiliar place asking.... *how did I get here?*

Are you lost in the valley of depression and stress and saying...*I'm tired of being here!*

"Faith must always pass the test of discouragement. Faith becomes a bridge between where I am and where I want to go - it is a substance.

You are not going to defeat the devil with will power - you need the power of God and if you lose your faith you've lost the fight.

You have to recognize as troubles, trials and tests come into your life, you have to recognize that there is a God who sits high and looks low and has all power and has all power in His hand and if you want to communicate with the divine... you do it by faith. "

~ Bishop T. D. Jakes

You may be feeling stuck and procrastinating when it comes to continuing and completing your project, exercising, college, weight loss, increasing your savings, building your business, seeking a job, buying a home or self-control to stay clean and sober.

E*motions* of defeat can paralyze your **motion**.

You may not "feel" like doing what you need to do.

A great definition for "discipline" is ...do what you don't want to do now --- so you can do what you want to do in the future.

Get up. Motivate yourself. Press on, persist, persevere and push past your pain and discomfort.

Life is so precious. Life is too short to sit around having a pity party, sleeping your time away, vegetating in front of the TV, complaining or living with excuses or lack of knowledge. Get up. Step up. Think up. Cheer up. Stand up. Grow up. Pray up. Reach up. Stir up your gifts. Speak up. Keep up and don't give up.

"Do not wait; the time will never be "just right." Start where you stand, and work with whatever tools you may have at your command, and better tools will be found as you go along." -- Napoleon Hill

Are you easily discouraged?

Abraham **(Abe)** Lincoln's "Failures" List

Lost job in 1832.
Defeated for state legislature in 1832.
Failed in business in 1833.
Elected to state legislature in 1834.
Sweetheart died in 1835.
Had nervous breakdown in 1836.
Defeated for Speaker in 1838.
Defeated for nomination for Congress in 1843.
Elected to Congress in 1846.
Lost re-nomination in 1848.
Rejected for land officer in 1849.
Defeated for U.S. Senate in 1854.
Defeated for nomination for Vice President in 1856.
Again defeated for U.S. Senate in 1858.
Elected President in 1860.

Abe Lincoln's journey is an example of not letting his failures to become a dis**abe**-lity or a stumbling block. These experiences became his stepping stones.

"Though I have fallen, I will rise.

Though I sit in darkness,

The Lord will be my light. ~ Micah 7:8

Whenever I have a difficult and stressful day, I go to sleep... and the next morning ... I place my feet on the floor and rise again, undefeated, so I can make enemy say....

"Darn...she's up again !"

And let us not he weary in well doing

for in due season

we shall reap, if we faint not. -- Galatians 6:9

You may not like where you are now, but this is not your final destination ... unless you give up and sit down.

Depression is a set up to make you give up. Don't let the enemy shut your mouth, steal your health, faith, praise peace of mind or destiny.

S omeone can love you,

but you must make yourself happy.

❖ Someone can teach you,

but you must apply what you learn.

❖ Someone can coach you,

but you must win the game.

❖ Someone can give you an opportunity,

but you must be capable and prepared.

❖ Someone can give you truth or lies,

but you must learn discernment.

❖ Someone can tempt you,

but you must learn discipline.

❖ Someone can offer you advice,

but you must learn to trust your own

inner knowing.

❖ Someone else can withhold,

but you must learn to give.

❖ Someone can pity you,

but you must bear your own sorrow.

❖ Someone can leave you,

       but you must learn to feel whole.

❖ Someone can set you up or put you down,

       but you must still do the right thing.

❖ Someone can knock you down,

       but you must get back up.

❖ Someone can ignore you,

       but you must see your own value and worth.

❖ Someone can help you,

       but you must learn to do for self.

❖ Someone can hold a grudge,

       but you must learn how to forgive.

❖ Someone can show you a new way,

       but you must want the change.

❖ Someone can love you,

       but you must feel worthy of receiving love.

❖ Someone can inspire you,

       but you must motivate yourself.

My motto was always to keep swinging. Whether I was in a slump or feeling badly or having trouble off the field, the only thing to do was keep swinging.   ~ **Hank Aaron**

Losing doesn't eat at me the way it used to. I just get ready for the next play, the next game and the next season.

~ **Troy Aikman**

My father...made us shop at Goodwill. I found things to wear and got Best Dressed (in the yearbook) two years in a row. I had lemons, so I made lemonade.

~ **Nick Cannon**

"Surround yourself with only people who are going to lift you higher. You will be wounded many times in your life. You'll make mistakes. Some people will call them failures but I have learned that failure is really God's way of saying, "Excuse me, you're moving in the wrong direction." It's just an experience, just an experience." ~ **Oprah Winfrey**

"In order to reach your goal you must continue to strive in spite of interference or treatment."

~ **Harriett Tubman**

"Don't sit down and wait for the opportunities to come. Get up and make them! " ~ **Madame C. J. Walker**

In the book, *It's About Time*, authors Sapadin and Maguire classified procrastinators into six types:

The "**perfectionist**" - dreads doing anything that is less than perfect, it has to be all or nothing at all.

The "**dreamer**" – is a pleasure seeker, enjoys kicking back and relaxing, hates dealing details.

The "**worrier**" - doesn't think things are right but fears that changes will make them worse.

The "**defier**" - angry, rebels and resists doing any thing suggested or expected by someone else.

The "**crisis-maker**" – finds or creates a big problem in any project (often by starting too late).

The "**over-doer**" - takes on far too many tasks and doesn't know how to delegate or prioritize.

Are you a "wait watcher?"

You can lose the "wait habit" and "weight" from the build up of unfinished tasks. Learn to classify your tasks as _urgent_ or <u>priority</u>. Don't just give attention to "**comfort**" tasks which are more convenient, interesting and fun. Priority is sacrificed for convenience. Consequently, other tasks begin to pile up. Procrastination and stress are set into motion because of the backlog of unfinished tasks.

Are your dreams on hold while you wait for every thing to be perfect or other people to help and encourage you? Three common reasons you may never fulfill your dreams:

1. The picture is fuzzy. You are **not clear** and specific about your dream/purpose?

2. You know exactly what you want, but you think it's impossible. It's **just a dream** not a goal.

3. You know what you want, but **lack the courage, self-esteem** and **faith** to pursue it.

If you suffer from the "_disease to please_", trying to do everything for everybody will drain you, drive you crazy and drive you further away from your own important tasks and needs. Healthy and productive **emotional boundaries** are set when you can say "no" without explanation or guilt.

Speak more positively.   Suggested positive-talk language:

I trust myself to do the right thing.

My life is getting better and better each day.

Setting and achieving goals is fun and productive.

I am taking responsibility for the quality of my life.

I am driven by a sense of purpose.

I use my time, talent and treasures wisely.

I am ready to commit to my goal.

I focus my efforts on things that are important.

I am deserving and worthy of success.

I am well able to finish what I start.

I am excited about my possibilities for success.

I can do this!

If you are avoiding taking action on something difficult or different, rehearse it in your imagination or with someone.

Walk through the scenario in your mind visualizing a positive outcome.   Visualize yourself passing the test, closing the sale, graduating, performing in front of an audience, opening the door to your new home or getting the job.

Listen to the excuses you give to others and to yourself. Procrastinators are good *self con artists* because they can sell themselves a great lie to justify avoiding critical action. They avoid taking action by telling themselves...

"I'll do it tomorrow"

"I do my best work late at night, I'll do it then."

"I'll call them just as soon as I think of something clever to say."

"I'll need to paint and get new furniture before inviting family and friends over."

"There's no need in taking that test again, I know I'll just fail and be embarrassed again."

"If I'm late, they won't mind."

"If I can't finish it, I'm sure someone will help me."

"I can't do it now. I need to wait until everyone supports and believes in me. I don't handle confusion and confrontation well. It's best to wait until everyone is on board with me."

Do **un**pleasant tasks first and get them out of the way.

Do you work better in solitude? Don't be afraid to ask family, friends or co-workers for their support by honoring your privacy to work on a project. It's better to communicate your needs than to suffer from frustration, stagnation and moodiness.

Accept the fact that you will never be "in the mood" to do some things. Maturity and discipline are evident when you rise above ambivalent feelings and take responsibility, regardless of how tempting it is to wait until tomorrow.

Some people sabotage their success and progress because they don't want negative attention or they don't know how to respond to positive attention. Procrastination is a form of sabotage.

Do you deny or unconsciously avoid success? Accept compliments about your work performance by simply saying, *"Thank you."*

Figure out why you feel uncomfortable with success. Did someone in your life make you feel that way? Were you taught to minimize your success? Why is success so frightening? Will it make you stand out in the crowd?

If you are successful, do you feel as though others will criticize you?

Set up a contract with someone to help you stay on track until completion of your pre-determined and clear goal. Being accountable to someone helps to reduce any excuses or further avoidance.

◉

It may be motivating to scare yourself a little. Think about this... What will happen if you don't take action? (i.e. taxes, doctor appointment, college classes, pay bills on time, traffic tickets, make your sales calls, etc.)

What will be your painful and costly consequences from your lack of action?

The people in your life have an influence on you. If you spend too much time with people who are unsupportive, lack ambition or people who don't share your same goals and lifestyle, you will soon be too discouraged or lose interest in achieving your goals. Upgrading and enlarging your circle of influences can take your life to the next level.

◉

Fatigue can cause you to stop and put things off. Take short breaks to re-energize your self. Most people don't realize that their bodies are dehydrated. Your brain needs water to function well. Sugar and caffeine only provide false bursts of energy. Improve your nutrition and water intake and you will gain so much energy. Drinking plenty of water each day energizes your body.

⊙

what you're going to do to everyone. _ about what you're going to do month after month and year after year is often another avoidance tactic.

Talk is cheap, it's time to leap. **Just do it.**

Create your treasure map. Collect pictures of your goals i.e. *car, vacation, home, furniture, role models, exercise equipment, office equipment, etc.*

Remain focused on completion of tasks by keeping your goals and list of *things to do* visible. If they are out of sight, they are out of mind.

Notice the time wasters in your life (i. e. *TV, computer, telephone, playing ball, helping other people, social invitations, sleeping too much, etc.)* There is a difference between being busy or being productive.

Stop wasting time and get busy. Procrastinators know how to avoid important tasks by starting new projects.

Don't spend major time on minor things.

Don't "over think" your steps. Paralysis of analysis happens when you are stuck in the *developing* stage of your goals instead of the *doing* stage. Only action produces satisfaction.

⊙

Self-absorption, self-pity and whining are selfish and non-productive. Let your loss of money, opportunities and time inspire you to change. Let your lessons be your **stepping stones** instead of stumbling blocks.

⊙

Embarrassment and self-esteem issues about your weight, lack of education and socio-economic status can be the cause of procrastination. A sense of shame from believing negative messages from hurtful people can make you a procrastinator. You could unknowingly sabotage your own success because you internalized the messages of shame, unworthiness and failure.

Feeling like a victim: helpless, powerless, worthless and incompetent Is a counter productive state of mind. Forgiveness, emotional and spiritual healing are important to remove the blockages of shame.

Counseling, reading, prayer, creative expression i.e., (*art, poetry, dancing, music, gardening, sports, painting, writing, helping and serving others*) are helpful ways to stimulate your imagination and emotional well-being.

Learn ways to restore your sense of value and hope.

Get un-stuck !

Stop suffering from paralysis of analysis.   Stop the "*all or nothing*" approach.   Perfectionism is strongly related to depression and an extremely critical concept of self or other people.

Read with a pen in your hand, and enter in a journal the thoughts that peak your interest or that

might be useful both now and in

the future. Keep paper and pen

near your bed side to capture the

flow of creativity and things to do.

Have a list of:

- ✓ things to **do** today
- ✓ things to **accomplish** this month, this year, etc.
- ✓ things to **discard**
- ✓ things to **delegate**
- ✓ things to **dare and dream**

Journaling helps you work through challenges and opportunities without the fear of social consequences. Writing can help you dream and live outside the box of your comfort zone. You can journal about things that you don't want to discuss with friends or family.

Journaling is a great way to be creative and heal old emotional wounds that may be blocking your blessings.

A blank page is a safe place to experiment with ideas that on the surface would seem far outside the realm of possibility.

Success **first** starts in your mind and then your behind must get up and take action. Give thanks to God **before** you even see the manifestation. Gratitude is a great attitude for goal GETTING!

Get out of your holding pattern of procrastination and fear. Take your happiness out of the "lay- away." Find your strength, integrity and courage. Find your voice. Trust your decisions. Learn from your choices. Use your imagination. Trust your instincts. Pray for guidance and discernment. Explore your ideas. Walk by faith. Action speaks louder than fear. You are enough!

Procrastination is a thief stealing your money, time and peace of mind. Avoiding tasks, tardiness and disorganization make you ineffective, creates stress and blocks success. If you need to finish a task, what is your habit?

✦ **Delay,** reschedule and postpone.

✦ **Delegate** to someone so you are free to focus on your priorities.

✦ **Don't know how to plan** and prioritize, paralyzed by fear.

✦ **Denial** , "It's not that bad, it will go away."

✦ **Distracted** focusing on easier or fun things to do.

✦ **Dependent** on someone to do it for you.

✦ **Defiant**, angry and rebellious, feeling life and people are not fair.

✦ **Dump** on others, run from responsibilities because you are afraid, lazy, inexperienced or immature.

✦ **Drag** your feet, dilly-dally and **defer** it until an indefinite time.

✦ **Desire** perfection and guarantees.

✦ **Do it** - get it done, face the fear, seize the moment, ask for help, experience relief, results and progress.

What are you avoiding?

Let this be the day you decide to stop procrastinating, hesitating, stressing, blaming, avoiding or focusing on non-productive activity. Procrastination is birthed from fear.

Fear is a faith killer. Fear robs you of your peace of mind. Fear blocks your blessings. Self-esteem comes from knowing you're making the effort to grow. If you are making your best effort, you can live with a deep sense of satisfaction.

Remember these important steps to achieve your goals:

- Write down clear and specific goals.
- Focus on progress, not perfection.
- Ask for help and accountability.
- Associate with people who can push you up your mountain.
- Pray for strength, courage and discipline.
- Think big. What you see --- is what you get. Visualize your success.
- Discernment is critical. Guard your goals. Don't talk about them to everyone.
- Train your brain for success. Read and listen to messages to keep you moving beyond *momentary* motivation.
- Obstacles, distractions and delays will happen. Pump up your determination, optimism and your "**I can**" attitude.
- Keep the main thing....THE MAIN THING! Don't give up.

Procrastination has painful and costly consequences. The avoidance habit interferes with your professional, personal and financial success.

Procrastination diminishes your credibility. Consistent and positive behavior builds trust, integrity and self-esteem.

Whatever you plant in our **subconscious mind** and nourish with repetition and emotion will one day become a reality.

If you do nothing --- nothing happens. Once you are disciplined to focus on your direction and priorities, you can make your goals a reality.

Your success does not always depend on how smart or how talented you are. It's about your ability to; communicate and work with others, your tenacity, passion, consistency, creativity, credibility, associations, determination, honesty, professionalism and faith.

Write the following statement down to motivate yourself when you feel; like giving up, procrastinating, impatient, blaming and making excuses.

"If I do nothing --- nothing happens."

"You must maintain unwavering faith that you can and will prevail in the end, regardless of the difficulties, *AND at the same time* have the discipline to confront the most brutal facts of your current reality, whatever they might be."

~ Jim Collins, author of "Built to Last"

Distractions are a huge drain on every aspect of who we are. It takes your focus away from what we should be doing - our tasks, goals and purpose. Learn how to eliminate them from your life!

Once you learn the skill of concentration and follow through, nothing and no one can stop you from achieving anything!

Right now you are probably spending a lot of energy trying to avoid pain or gain pleasure in life.

When pain is associated with doing a particular task, the procrastination increases. It's in our human nature to run away from things which cause us pain.

When you start to associate a payoff/reward with a task, the momentum of action steps will increase.

We all know that in order to accomplish a certain thing we must concentrate. It is of the utmost value to learn how to concentrate. To make a success of anything you must be able to concentrate your entire thought upon the idea you are working out. When it comes to any activity or attitude, balance is critical. Focused concentration is a good mindset, yet you want to remember to spend time with the people and interests that bring you joy and happiness. Focused attention is in vain if you don't have balance. If you're too busy and focused on your business or any project to make time for your family, friends, relaxation and spiritual growth, then your focus may be too obsessive. The mind **does not** like discipline and will resist your efforts to discipline it. Your mind remembers your past start-and-stop habits. Your mind has a guard protecting past memories and habits. When you attempt to introduce new ideas and new habits, your ego mind will resist them. It loves its freedom more than anything else, and will try to stand in your way to master it, in any way it can. It will cause you to forget, postpone and make excuses. It will find many tricks to stop and disturb you, but you can and must be stronger. Repetition and good feelings about your new ideas and habits are the keys that open the door to your unconscious mind. Eventually the guard will allow new ideas in because your consistency is a persistent knock on the door that has been closed.

You may not love exercising, studying, drinking more water or making sales calls. Attention is always highly selective. We always find time for the people and activities we value and love. If you love and value your health, family, income, freedom, love and peace of mind --- then begin to place a high priority on those tasks. Energy flows where your attention goes. You can achieve the goal you highly value because it holds your concentrated attention.

Small value – small attention.

Big value – big attention.

Small attention – small energy.

Big attention – big energy.

Small faith – small power

Intent shapes your attracting power. If you are procrastinating or lack concentration to keep the main thing...the main thing – could it be you don't value or love performing that task? Well, my friend, remember the loss and consequences if you don't learn how to concentrate placing attention on your intentions to follow through on your goals, tasks and dreams. If you value them, you can start today taking action. If they are not that important, then start focusing on what is important. What do you really value? Is it your health, income, peace of mind, weight loss, marriage, spirituality, business building, writing a book, sobriety, spending time with your family, retirement, sports, graduation, community, church, traveling, retirement, etc.

Make a decision to follow your vision.   Take action.

Examine all the options that are immediately open to you. In other words, weigh the pros and cons of each possibility but don't confuse yourself with too many choices.

Reduce the possibility of interruptions.

A wandering mind easily falls into temptation.

Learn how to overcome dullness, agitation, unclear goals, and an overwhelming schedule of demands.

Conquer the little things, so the little things don't become big things.

If you can't handle and manage the small things in life, you're not ready to master the big things. This is scriptural. Read Luke 16:10

⊙

"Never, never think outside the box!"

Constructive advice and guidance from informed people can be extremely helpful in saving a great deal of time and energy. However, be very careful at the early stages about who you take into your confidence. You can't afford to tell everyone about your goals. Criticism and jealousy can cause you to stop. Your thinking "outside the box" can seem radical, crazy and risky to some people. *Left brain thinkers* do not generally like to take risks. Their mind seeks a life that is safe, predictable, organized and structured. Every one in your circle of family, friends and co-workers will not always encourage you to break away from the pack of the ordinary and average. If you tend to be a *right brain thinker* you are more likely to be adventurous, curious, spontaneous and willing to take risks. On one hand that is a great recipe for travelers, entrepreneurs, artists and creative people. However, when it comes to focusing on a goal and completing a task, *right brain thinkers* need to train their brain to stick with a task until it's completed.

> Guard your goals.

If you are experiencing a mental overload, you will find it difficult to stay organized, set priorities, and manage time. Take a break, take a deep breath and allow your self to reflect and regroup. Rid your environment of clutter. Delegate tasks. Focus on your urgent and priority tasks first. Be sure to get my **CD** "The Main Thing is to Keep the Main Thing...THE MAIN THING."

Also, be reminded to avoid being overly driven for success. Don't push yourself so hard that you lose your life balance and health. A big lesson I have learned, with my success driven and superwoman personality, is that it is OK to ask for help. It is not a sign of weakness. Don't allow your pride or need for privacy keep you burdened and ineffective.

"The most valuable opportunities are often overlooked because they first appear much smaller than most people expect. Yet they are easily spotted by those who understand that seeing the opportunity is just the beginning. The biggest opportunities are hidden in the smallest moments. See them, understand them, make use of them, and they can lift you to incredible heights. "

-- Ralph Marston

"The victory of success is half won when one gains the habit of setting goals and achieving them. Even the most tedious chore will become endurable as you parade through each day convinced that every task, no matter how menial or boring, brings you closer to fulfilling your dreams."   **~ Og Mandino**

"You have to think anyway, so why not think BIG."

~ Donald Trump

"You have to find something that you love enough to be able to take   risks, jump over the hurdles and break through the brick walls that are always going to be placed in front of you. If you don't have that kind of feeling for what it is you are doing, you'll stop at the first giant hurdle."

~ George Lucas, Film Director and Producer

"Develop a mentor at each stage of your career – someone who will give you guidance and advice."

~ Brian Tracy

"We become what we think about all day long."

~ Ralph Waldo Emerson

"We tend to get what we expect."

~ Norman Vincent Peale

"Whether you think you can or think you can't, you are right".   **~ Henry Ford**

"Whatever your mind can conceive and believe, it can achieve."   **~ Napoleon Hill**

"Those who follow the crowd are quickly lost in it."

~ Anonymous

"Well done is better than well said."

~ Benjamin Franklin

"A good goal is like a strenuous exercise -- it makes you stretch."   **~ Mary Kay Ash**

"The ultimate measure of a man is not where he stands in moments of comfort and convenience, but where he stands at times of challenge and controversy."

~ Dr. Martin Luther King, Jr.

"Success is to be measured not so much by the position that one has reached in life, as by the obstacles one has overcome trying to succeed."

~ Booker T. Washington

"Nothing can stop the man with the right mental attitude from achieving his goal; nothing on earth   can help the man with the wrong mental attitude."

~ W.W. Ziege

"Do not let the hero in your soul perish, in lonely frustration for the life you deserved, but have never been able to reach. Check your road and the nature of your battle. The world you desired can be won. It exists, it is real, it is possible, it is yours."

~ Ayn Rand

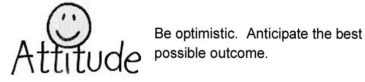 Be optimistic. Anticipate the best possible outcome.

The word *optimism* is derived from Latin *ops meaning* power.

Hope is essential to a vital life. Your happiness or your misery depends upon what you tell yourself, how you treat yourself and how you interpret your world.

Your thoughts and habits determine which path you take in life.

What do you think about all day?

Your thoughts determine your destiny.

Your **behind follows** your **mind.**

If you don't like the direction of your life, change your thoughts.

Wake up the sleeping giant **inside of you.** Activate the power within you. Your words, thoughts, prayers and actions **have power.**

Snap out of any depression.

Wake up! Get up!

Your words, feelings and thoughts are like a magnet.

You **attract** into your life;

what you **expect**,

what you **fear**,

what you **give thanks** for,

what you **believe**,

what you feel **worthy** of receiving,

what you **act** upon on,

what you **concentrate** on,

what you *visualize*,

what you **talk** about,

what you **prepare** for,

and what you **think** about all day.

No matter how good or how right you are, the reality is that some people don't want to see you shine. The enemy to your success will try to confuse you and resent your progress and talents. You may have to work harder to prove yourself because of your gender, race, age, education, achievements, family, friends, talent, gifts, charisma, favor, social standing or your looks. It's not fair, but it happens.

Procrastination is a thief !

"If you're **proactive, you focus** on **preparing**. If you're **reactive**, you end up focusing on **repairing**. When you invest in today… it's like putting money in the bank. It's like studying for the test tomorrow. You're just better prepared to meet life's challenges."

~ John C. Maxwell

Learn to bounce back from your setbacks and disappointments.

Get up!

Perfectionism and self-criticism can be so abusive and non-productive.

Don't be too hard on yourself... yet continue to push yourself towards the next level of improvement.

There may be times you may **not** "feel" like doing what you should do; **i.e.** balance your budget, exercise, school work, build your business, get over the blues or fight the battle of the bulge, clear out the clutter in your office, closet, garage, car, etc. Feelings of apathy, indifference, denial, procrastination, fear and doubt **do not serve you well**.

Going to the next level in your life requires action above and beyond how you feel. Doing something consistently removes distraction and doubt. Success will happen for you when you can discipline yourself.

The key to success and growth is the ability to do what you should do, when you should do it, whether you like it or not. Study successful people and you will see they have discipline and are willing to pay the price when others don't feel like it. They go the extra mile. They put in the extra time and they have a "*made up mind*."

 Finding shoes in my closet that I had not seen or worn in a long time reminded me of a success principle...

"If it's out of sight, it's out of mind."

Where is your list of goals written down?

What do you want to accomplish today, this week, this year...5 years from now?

You will place more attention on your intentions when they are in constant view. If not, you can be easily discouraged and distracted.

Give your mind an assignment and your behind will follow.

You will see more results as you practice the habit of writing down your short term and long term goals for successful living.

Think and **ink** your goals.

Be specific.

Review them often.

Take consistent action.

"Each of us should do something every day that we do not want to do ... but we know we should do, to strengthen our backbone and put iron in our soul. "

~ Henry Hitt Crane

"There is a place that you are to fill and no one else can fill, something you are to do, which no one else can do."
~ *Plato, The Divine Design*

"Man must prepare for the thing he has asked for, even where there isn't the slightest sign of it in sight."

~ Florence Scovel Shinn

"Calmness of the mind is one of the beautiful jewels of wisdom." ~ **William James**

"Life is like a game of chess... there are many moves possible, but each move determines your next move... where you wind up is the sum total of your past moves...but first you have to make some kind of move."

~ **Mort Walker**

"Life moves pretty fast. If you don't stop and look around once in a while you could miss it."

~ From the movie *Ferris Bueller's Day Off*

Not everyone deserves a front row seat in your **theater of life.** Real friends don't come with a "fragile" sticker and are not easily scared off, turned off or ticked off.

"Champions aren't made in gyms. Champions are made from something they have deep inside them – a desire, a dream, a vision. They have last minute stamina. They have to be a little faster. They have to have the skill and the will. But the **will** must be stronger than the skill."

~ **Muhammad Ali**

*"So teach us to make the most of our time so that we may grow in wisdom." ~ **Psalm 90:12***

"Until one is committed, there is hesitancy, the chance to draw back, always ineffectiveness. Concerning all acts of initiative (and creation), there is one elementary truth the ignorance of which kills countless ideas and splendid plans.

The moment one definitely commits oneself, then providence moves too. All sorts of things occur to help   one that would never otherwise have occurred.

A whole stream of events issues from the decision, raising in one's favor all manner of unforeseen incidents and meetings and material assistance, which no man could have dreamed would have come his way. Whatever you can do, or dream you can, begin it. Boldness has genius, power and magic in it. Begin it now." ~ **Goethe**

Your opportunities can come from the most unexpected places.

· **Ask** for what you want.

· **Act** on what you want.

· **Affirm** what you want.

· **Actualize** what you want.

Focus today on solutions, peace, love, right action, right speech and right thinking.

What do you want to accomplish?

Keep the main thing...**the MAIN THING**!

Nobody is going to care as much about your success and "wants" in life as much as you do.

Procrastination is a passive decision to do nothing.

Change **before** you have to change. Start changing your poor habits into wiser habits before life offers you **no more** time, no more second chances or no more grace and mercy.

Pray for discernment. Listen and obey spiritual guidance. Discipline your weaknesses and addictions.

Practice patience and perseverance and you will reap the abundant, healthy and peaceful life.

Are you choosing change or change is choosing you. The mystery and beauty of life is that you will experience beauty, emptiness, pain, joy, fear, love, loss, success, change, surprises, disappointments, interruptions, uncertainty and moments of clarity. The western mind demands answers for every thing. We want control over our circumstances and even people. Wisdom gained teaches that you only have control of your response to change and your coping skills.

I surrender to the flow of change.

I trust myself to adjust to change.

I am willing to explore new options.

I embrace new adventures.

I am responsibility for the quality of my future.

I am capable to make new decisions.

I am proactive.

Notice the time wasters in your life. There is a difference between being busy or being productive. Stop wasting time and get busy. Procrastinators know how to avoid important tasks by starting new projects. **Don't spend major time on minor things.**

Don't allow past blunders to blur your vision for victory. You are smarter than you give yourself credit for.

You are a creative problem solver.

Put on your thinking cap.

- **C** - concentrate without distractions, focus
- **A** - affirm the positive, be optimistic.
- **P** - pray for discernment, wisdom and courage. Proverbs 3:6 teaches, "In all your ways acknowledge Him, and He will direct your paths."

"Somehow I can't believe there are any heights that can't be achieved by men who know the secret of making dreams come true. This special secret, it seems to me, can be summarized in four C's. They are Curiosity, Confidence, Courage, and Constancy, and the greatest of these is Confidence. When you believe a thing, believe in it all the way."

~ Walt Disney

◆

"Through wisdom is a house built, and by understanding,   it is established; and by knowledge shall the chambers be filled with precious and pleasant riches."   **Proverbs 24: 3-4**

◆

"Winners don't just rely on skill power, they have will power. Winners don't make excuses, they make a way. Winners don't give up, they get up! **Winners don't complain...they train.** Winners get equipped so they can't be whipped by the setbacks, hurdles and fumbles in of life. Only the strong survive. You cannot live with fear and faith at the same time."

~ Jewel Diamond Taylor

When bad stuff happens you can develop a new perspective. Instead of thinking that life is punishing you... could it be **pushing** you to grow stronger in another direction?

You can either sit with your confusion and pain or you can choose to focus on new possibilities and inner peace. You can either focus on the question, "Why did this happen?" Or you can focus on the question, "What do I need to do next?"

I've seen in my own life and in others how fear of change can cause us to shut down, hold back, isolate, medicate, procrastinate, hibernate, play the blame game, become sick, stressed, panic and close our hearts and minds. Fear causes us to feel miserable, angry, vulnerable and like a hopeless victim. A mind full of fear has tunnel vision focusing only on the door that closed. Fear never allows us to see the other doors of possibilities. We have so much fear of not being in control, of not being able to hold on to things. Yet the true nature of things is that you're never in control. You can learn how to control your response to change. You can never hold on to anything. Life doesn't always make sense or make us feel safe and comfortable.

We're used to running from discomfort. If we don't like it, we strike out at someone or beat up on ourselves with guilt, fear and gloom. We want to have security and certainty of some kind. On the path of life you will experience change, loss, grief and unexpected detours and bumps. Reading this message can nurture your faith and create a proactive mindset. This message can help you develop emotional and *spiritual shock absorbers* for the changes and bumps in life. Only the strong survive and thrive through the many kinds of life changes.

To cope with change, I've learned to stay awake instead of numbing myself, blaming or turning in the opposite direction. Walking by faith and not by sight is an attitude that helps me to develop a spirit of hope, a mind of possibilities and a heart of joy and gratitude. Nothing in life is permanent or guaranteed. No one is immune from misfortune. Life is precious and unpredictable. Life is bitter and life is sweet. You live in a world full of good and bad, joy and pain, ups and downs and turnarounds. When life shakes and wakes you up, you can make yourself miserable or you discover meaning.

This book is a tool to help cultivate your mind with seeds of hope, peace and adaptability. Give yourself the *success advantage* by revisiting the book often.

The path to success is not straight.

You cannot control the weather.

You must carry your own map.

There are roadblocks

called disappointment.

There are caution speed bumps

called friends.

There are red lights called enemies.

There are caution lights called family.

There are tempting detours along the way.

There are curves called change. You will have flat tires, but if you have: a spare tire called determination, an engine called perseverance and faith, a vehicle called good health, insurance called grace and mercy, friends and mentors as fellow passengers, your purpose and goals as your compass, and the Lord as your navigator, you will have strength for your journey and you will reach your destination.

The mystery *and* beauty of life is that you will experience emptiness, pain, joy, fear, love, loss, success, change, surprises, disappointments, uncertainty and moments of clarity. The western mind demands answers for every thing. Remember to enjoy the beauty and blessings this day offers. We want control over our circumstances and even people. Wisdom teaches that you only have control of your response to change and your coping skills.

I have discovered several ways people cope or respond to unwanted life changes. Because you are a creature of habit, you have a tendency to act, think and respond in the same way when life throws you a curve ball.

Which of the following responses is your dominant coping pattern when faced with difficult life changes?

1. **antagonistic** (become rebellious, argumentative, nasty, bitter, resentful, quarrelsome and counterproductive)
2. **act out** (reckless, loud, aggressive and feeling like a victim)
3. **alienation** (remote, withdraw, no communication)
4. **avoidance** (denial, bypass, skirt around the issue)
5. **anger** (enraged, irritable, blood pressure escalates)
5. **apathy** (indifferent, don't care, no point in doing anything)
6. **allowance** (tolerate bad situations feeling hopeless or afraid to be confrontational.)
7. **accusations** (blame and point fingers, taking no responsibility)
8. **adapt** (make appropriate adjustments, have a plan B)
9. **acceptance** (choosing peace about those things which you have no control, prayer, let go of the resistance)
10. **action** steps (proactive, what's my next step?)

As a long-time prisoner in the concentration camps Viktor Frankl found himself stripped to naked existence. His father, mother, brother, and his wife died in camps or were sent to gas ovens, so that, excepting for his sister, his entire family perished in these camps. How could he every possession lost, every value destroyed, suffering from hunger, cold and brutality, hourly expecting extermination - how could he find life worth living after so many changes and loss?" Viktor Frankl's mindset was…*"The one thing you can't take away from me is the way I choose to respond to what you do to me. The last of one's freedoms is to choose ones attitude in any given circumstance. When we are no longer able to change a situation - we are challenged to change ourselves."*

Life has a way of waking us up from a false sense of security and predictability.   The seasons of loss and change in my life were not as tragic as Victor Frankl, none the less, I had to learn how to cope.

My first fight with God happened when my mother lost her battle with breast cancer in 1985. In spite of the prayers, denial and bargaining with God, I became a Motherless child. I wasn't prepared for that type of change, pain and loss in my life.

Since that dark time, I've had many more experiences of dealing with unwelcome change, uncertainty, surprises and transitions. I grew to understand what the stage play "Your Arms Are Too Short to Box with God" really meant. I have resisted change and had many more spiritual battles with God. I've grown now to understand over the years that I didn't lose the fights... I learned tremendous life lessons. I discovered a peace and inner strength to go on that I never knew was in me.

Sometimes you will choose change and sometimes change *chooses you*. Change is a basic law of nature. We struggle when it reshapes the familiar and breaks up the continuity in our lives. Change can bring growth or grief. Change can be minor, radical, life altering, exciting, challenging, even frightening, but it can also be managed.

Change has taught me many lessons; I didn't like change when my parents passed away, learning to adjust to the empty nest of my sons moving out on their own, disappointed when a big speaking contract was cancelled and when a TV producer changed their mind about my opportunity to be a life coach on a popular TV show, changes in my body, changes in the world as result of terrorism, in schools, technology, war and economy.

I've seen changes in my marriage 'and family, some pleasant and some sad. Old friends have left and new friends have enriched my life. Change is something I have learned to grow with, endure and enjoy. Change is not always fair, convenient, comfortable, predictable or controlled.

What was happy can turn to sad, things get rearranged and nothing stays the same. You *cannot* always choose the changes that come your way. But you can always choose your response. Whether you are facing an empty nest, life after divorce, a new city, change in your health or a change in your daily job policy and procedures, change in weather or a change of heart from a friend/lover/spouse, learn to adapt rather than be a victim of change.

It's easy to have faith and a positive state of mind when everything is going right in your life. Life can change without your permission and without notice.

You could be experiencing a change or loss in your life *i.e. layoff, divorce, business in a slump, death of a loved one, home destroyed in a fire or hurricane, surgery, car accident, taking care of an elderly parent or a new boss/new job or new city that you don't like.*

Depending upon your faith, coping skills and ability to adjust through changes, you will experience short or long emotional stages of shock, anger, grief, denial and even bargaining with God before you experience acceptance.

You can either choose to:

✦ **Suppress** your feelings (denial, fear, procrastination)

✦ **Digress** (lose clarity, resort back to old bad habits)

✦ Become **stressed** (angry, sick, resentful)

✦ **Depress** your feelings (addictions, sleep, depression)

✦ **Obsess** (preoccupied in the negative grip of fear)

✦ **Decompress** (breath, exercise, sports, dance, relax)

✦ **Confess** (speak about it, seek help and support)

✦ **Bless** the mess (pray about it, let go and Let God)

✦ **Express** your feelings in a healthy way without anger, blame, shame and defeat.

We are given changes all the time. When we feel squeezed, there's a tendency for the mind to become small. We feel miserable, like a victim, like a pathetic, hopeless case.

We have so much fear of not being in control, of not being able to hold on to things. Yet the true nature of things is that you're never in control. You're never in control. You can never hold on to anything. That's the nature of how things are. But it's almost like it's in the genes of being born human that you can't accept that. You can buy it intellectually, but moment to moment it brings up a lot of panic and fear.

Fear causes you to shut down, hold back, isolate and close your heart and mind. The truth you believe and cling to makes you unavailable to hear anything new. When you have narrow faith vision, you can't see a new way.

As we awake and accept the reality of human existence, we become used to the fact that things shift and change. Life cannot always be managed. Life will change without your permission. Children grow, parents age, flights get cancelled, weather changes, pets wander off, water heaters rust, and jobs come and go.

We cry, point fingers, can't sleep, feel hopeless, angry, close our eyes not wanting to see or know the truth and become paralyzed with fear and give up. That is what the enemy wants us to do when change and pain show up in our lives. Get up!

We can be angry at what has happened to us or others, **without** abandoning our faith, praise, hope and gratitude.

There are so many lessons we can learn from our personal setbacks and from witnessing the human suffering of others. What a marvelous time to truly go beyond talking our faith and now to walk it, live it, show it and share it.

Every demonstration of kindness, courage, prayer and giving will make a positive difference.

Every moment you decide to get up and overcome the paralysis of fear, the isolation of shame and hopelessness and take action, you have victory. Small victories lead to big victories. Small steps lead to progress.

As we see life tragedies in the news, we can learn from them how to be resilient, caring, strong and create a sense of community. Life is sending us messages to make a paradigm shift from greed, individualism, war, excess, materialism, inadequate and dishonest leadership to a nation of love, faith, caring, integrity, community, personal strength and political intelligence.

You could be facing unemployment, divorce, sickness, grief, financial struggle and feeling lost and displaced. Only the strong survive! Whether you are facing minor or major changes and challenges in your life, gospel singer Marvin Sapp inspires us through his song, "this is not the time and this is not the place for giving up."

Lyrics to Marvin Sapp's song:

This is not the time for giving up.

This is not your place where you should be. You got to hold on.

You got to be strong. This is not the time to question your faith.

This is not your place of destiny. It's not the time or the place to throw in the towel. You gotta hold on.

You gotta be strong. Sometimes you win. Sometimes you lose. It's a part of life that everyone goes through. Sometimes there's joy. Sometimes there's pain. That's apart of God's plan. It is His own plan. This is not the time and the place. Just believe in the faith. Gotta learn how to wait. There's still hope for the hopeless. There's still life for the lifeless. God is a friend to the friendless. He'll give you peace and sweetness. There's help for the helpless. There is a home if you're homeless. He will mend your broken pieces and cause you to live and be blessed.   This is not the time or the place. Gotta learn how to wait.   Don't give up.

Sometimes change is needed but you want to hold on in spite of the writing on the wall. The need to change or let go can be obvious, inevitable and the signs are every where to be seen and heard. You may be resisting change with all your will in fear of the unknown or the need to have what's comfortable and familiar remain status quo.

A train could be coming your way warning you to stop procrastinating...stop being silent...stop closing your eyes...stop resisting the cycles of life...stop the craziness in your life...stop focusing your time and energy on the wrong priorities...stop allowing the enemy to trick you...stop focusing your time and energy on the wrong priorities... stop putting yourself in harm's way and get off the tracks!!

Or **un**expected change can hit you on the blind side and you say to yourself, *"I didn't even see that coming!"*

A big question is ..."Why do so many people stay on the tracks when they see a train coming?"

I think it's because individuals inherently despise change or they think they can control the train!

Those who are proactive, anticipate change, and act quickly, get off the tracks and become passengers on another train. Resisting by closing your eyes or sitting on the tracks is a dangerous position.

It's the responsibility of every individual to seek out the latest knowledge, laws, technologies, systems and methods regarding all relevant aspects of their life. One should surround themselves with the most informed people possible and share knowledge and wisdom openly and often. Being an informed and updated knowledge worker can make you a change agent rather than a change victim and greatly add to your value in the marketplace. This same theory applies to all aspects of life including health, wealth and the constant pursuit of a brighter future.

When you experience the pain of change, you could begin to think you'll never get through it. The discomfort and fear that change brings can blind your ability to see hope and stability again. As I think back, I'm so thankful for the remembrance of how God has delivered me from drama, debt, dilemmas, death of my loved ones and depression. It is inevitable that life will bring me more changes to cope with. It won't be easy. But I'm thankful I have learned the importance of prayer, patience, positive coping habits and knowing that time heals all things.

Once upon a time, there was a farmer in the central region of China. He didn't have a lot of money and, instead of a tractor, he used an old horse to plow his field.

One afternoon, while working in the field, the horse dropped dead. Everyone in the village said, "Oh, what a horrible thing to happen to you."

The farmer said simply, "We'll see." He was so at peace and so calm, that everyone in the village got together and, admiring his attitude, gave him a new horse as a gift.

Everyone's reaction now was, "What a lucky man." And the farmer said, "We'll see."

A couple days later, the new horse jumped a fence and ran away. Everyone in the village shook their heads and said, "What a poor fellow!"

The farmer smiled and said, "We'll see."

Eventually, the horse found his way home, and everyone again said, "What a fortunate man."
The farmer said, "We'll see."

Later in the year, the farmer's young boy went out riding on the horse and fell and broke his leg. Everyone in the village said, "What a shame for the poor boy." The farmer said, "We'll see."

Two days later, the army came into the village to draft new recruits. When they saw that the farmer's son had a broken leg, they decided not to recruit him.

Everyone said, "What a fortunate young man."
The farmer smiled again - and said "We'll see."

Moral of the story: There's no use in overreacting to the events and circumstances of our everyday lives. Many times what looks like a setback, may actually be a gift in disguise. And when our hearts are in the right place, all events and circumstances are gifts that we can learn valuable lessons from.

As Fra Giovanni once said, *"Everything we call a trial, a sorrow, or a duty, believe me... the gift is there and the wonder of an overshadowing presence."*

When you experience conflict, change, stress, pressure, grief, loss...**notice your pattern**. Do you become reactive, resentful, remorseful or responsive to change? Do you become scared, suspicious, sour, stressed, shocked, sad, feel shame or feel stuck in hopelessness?

What happens to you when circumstances in your life *turn left* instead of right? Do you feel left behind? Are you left putting things back together again alone?

Are you left feeling that life is unfair and God is punishing you? Are you left feeling confused, overwhelmed and scared? Are you left holding broken dreams, feeling bitter and bewildered?

You can make yourself sick, angry and depressed as you constantly think and debate about the outcomes in your life that cannot be changed or controlled. Make a list of the things you can change. Start there with action and a plan.

My intention with this book is to share encouragement and positive coping skills to empower you to "grow" through the changes of life.

Life brings pleasant surprises as well as surprises that you won't be ready for. Many of these won't be fair.

Life usually brings **four types of change**:

 Change you **expect** and **glad** about it.

(new baby, new job, new house)

 Change you **expect** and **not** glad about it.

(loss of a loved one, aging, empty nest, foreclosure)

 Change you **didn't expect** and **glad** about it.

(promotion, transfer, new friend, new love interest)

 Change you **didn't expect** and **not** glad about

it. (divorce, death of a loved one, layoff, flood,

fire, illness, hurricane, car accident)

Change is not always fair, convenient, predictable or controlled. You cannot always choose the changes that come your way. But you can always choose your response.

Accept the unchangeable which requires disciplined endurance and tolerance.

Change the changeable which requires faith, courage and disciplined action.

Adapt and leverage the changes and circumstances that affect you.

Once we recognize and accept the circumstances we can't change, then we should learn to change the way we respond to them. We can choose to stay in peace or fall to pieces.

Best seller author Scott Peck began his book, The Road Less Traveled with this statement…

"Life is difficult. This is a great truth, one of the greatest truths. It is a great truth because once we truly see this truth, we transcend it. Once we truly know that life is difficult, once we truly understand and accept it, then life is no longer difficult. Because once it has been accepted, the fact that life is difficult no longer matters."

 It is in community with others that you find a sense of family, form and faith to enjoy and endure the seasons of life. When you are socially active and your spiritual faith is strong you are less likely to engage in unhealthy or negative behavior. When you're isolated, you're more prone to over indulgence in eating, drinking and sleeping. The negative demons of fear, depression, addiction and indifference are able to attack your spirit and mind.

When you are going through the storms of life, you need an anchor to keep from drowning in your tears, misery and thoughts of hopelessness. Choose acceptance and action instead of anger, apathy and avoidance patterns.

In difficult moments, *seek* God.

In quiet moments, *worship* God.

In painful moments, *trust* God.

Every moment, *thank* God.

Positive coping skills are important when fear and worry take your breathe and joy away.

CPR = Choose a Positive Response

When stress or change happens in your life, you have a choice to express one of the following responses to cope, endure and enjoy my life:

. **Avoidance** (resistance, fear)

. **Anger** (which creates more stress and resistance)

. **Allow** it to continue (victimization)

. **Apathy** (depression, procrastination)

. **Adapt** (flexible, change, grow)

. **Acceptance** (peace, let it go)

. **Action** (faith, proactive, courage)

"It's not so much that we're afraid of change or so in love with the old ways, but it's that place *in between* that we fear . It's like being between trapezes. It's like the cartoon character Linus when his blanket is in the dryer. There's nothing to hold on to."

~ Marilyn Ferguson

Feelings of impatience and stress are a sign to re-evaluate your reactions to what you cannot control or a wake up call to change what you can control. Frustration happens when you think your life is out of control or you wish you could control others. It happens when you believe people or progress in your life are *not* moving along according to your script.

Negative emotional reactions get in your way. They color your perceptions and drastically reduce your ability to notice what the situation really is, and to plan your best course of action. **Be responsive rather than reactive.**

A great source of frustration is change in our **physical** body, **policies, people** or **procedures** implemented in the work place, church, organizations or family matters.

A course called "Beyond Change Management" offered at Boise State University teaches **the 8 most common reasons for resisting change are:**

1) People don't understand why the change is necessary.

2) People don't believe the "change" will work.

3) People believe the old way is better.

4) People are afraid that they themselves might fail.

5) People don't trust the motives of the change agent.

6) There is evidence that the old way works.

7) There is little or no evidence that the new way will work.

8) The pain associated with changing is greater than the pain of remaining the same.

People do not really resist a change, they resist *being* **changed, resist uncertainty** and **loss.**

You, your family members and co-workers can be difficult and resistant to change if there is a feeling of **losing:**

. **power**   . **time**

. **money**   . **love and respect**

. **attention, recognition, praise**

. **personal control and freedom**

. **one's identity and meaning**

In the later years leading up to the passing of my Stepfather, his attitude was very resistant, stubborn, and cranky. His pride and choices seemed to make no sense to me and my sisters. We wanted to be good caregivers. However, we finally realized he was resisting the change age brings. He no longer had his job and title (loss of praise, respect and meaning). He couldn't drive (loss of freedom). We acted like his parent (loss of control, privacy and identity). He was on a fixed income (loss of money and personal choices). Our Mother had passed away years before from breast cancer and he lived alone. His mental capacity was diminished and he felt paranoid and thought no one loved him anymore (loss of love). No wonder he was difficult. He had experienced life changing shift on many levels!

People either *resist or yield* to change (shift). To work with difficult people effectively, it's important to identify where they feel threatened by change and loss.

I f you are the one initiating change in your organization or family, your goal should be to plan the change as effectively as possible to **minimize the uncertainty.** If people are resisting change, it is because they do not believe it is necessary. In other words, not enough clear communication has taken place.

If you are a leader making changes, learn to **communicate the plan well** to reduce sabotage, misunderstandings and resistance. When making changes in your organization or family, communication should be clear, constant and honest.

"The first step toward change is awareness. The second step is acceptance." ~ Nathaniel Branden

Until the pain of holding onto the old ways is great enough, many people find it easier to do nothing than to face doing something new. That's why unfortunately many people stay in dysfunctional, dangerous, unhappy relationships and hold onto jobs they despise.

Is change causing you to fall to pieces or do you have the peace of God within that surpasses all understanding? Do you see the bigger picture or are you isolating your thoughts and energy on this turn in your life? Instead of things going right for you, has life made a left turn? What's your next step? What are you thinking and talking about all day? What are you preparing for? Are you frozen with fear? Are you paralyzed by your predicament?

One prepares for what one believes will happen. At the same time, that preparation makes it more likely that this particular future will happen. Ask yourself what future you would prefer.

Recommended listening – Jewel Diamond

Taylor's CD – "Preparation Before Elevation

Everybody gets hit with life changes. Everybody will experience some form of a life passage (*career change, health issue, mid-life crisis, death of a loved one, moving to a new city, caring for an elderly parent, divorce or a financial setback*).

You can learn to minimize the pain of change by strengthening your personal infrastructure and increasing your faith to endure and adapt to life changes.

Got a problem? Your reactions and thoughts affect your peace and ability to overcome obstacles. Do you **react** like this?....

. I hate what's happening.

. Focus on what's wrong.

. I can't help myself.

. Insist on my own way.

. Worry incessantly until I'm sick.

. Feel stuck, helpless and

  hopeless.

. Defend my point of view.

. Find blame and point fingers.

. Struggle and isolate.

. Go into denial and

  avoidance.

. Hurry to the next thing.

Death of your spouse
Divorce
Marital separation
Prison
War
Death of a family member
Personal injury, illness Violence
Marriage
Layoff or fired from your job
Marital reconciliation
Retirement
Major change in behavior of family member or friend

Or are you learning to be proactive, optimistic, confident and respond like this…

☼ Notice what is working and my habitual pattern.

☼ Breathe, pray, meditate and relax.

☼ Accept and adapt to changes.

☼ Do something different.

☼ Be willing to feel the truth.

☼ Turn on my creative intuitive mind.

☼ Seek support.

☼ Re-think your choices and point of view.

☼ Open my heart and mind to solutions.

☼ Seek out information and people to support me through the life passage of change.

☼ Give thanks in advance for the breakthrough and blessings that will come from this experience.

☼ Put forth my best effort. Change what I can.

☼ Let go and let God with the issues I cannot change or control.

There are many ways to respond to life's issues of change, pain and obstacles.

- ✓ You could face it.

- ✓ You could avoid it.

- ✓ You could get angry and hate it. @#!%@*!

- ✓ You could look at it from a different perspective.

- ✓ You could see it as a gift.

- ✓ You could see it as a mystery.

- ✓ You could discover how strong you really are.

- ✓ You could experience a deepening of your faith.

- ✓ You could ask others for advice and support.

- ✓ You gained a life lesson.

- ✓ You could embrace and enjoy the experience.

- ✓ You could gain new insights about yourself and others around you.

- ✓ You could dramatize and exaggerate it.

- ✓ I could pray about it and surrender it all to God.

 You can think it is a small
problem and
procrastinate.

You can worry
and attract more
problems.

You can take action.

You could get over
it.

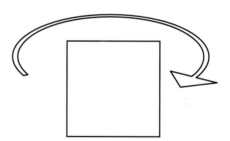

You can grow through it.

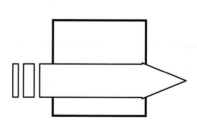

The language of "Denial"

This change doesn't really affect me.

The reality of the change hasn't set in yet.

This can't be happening now.

I'm not wasting my time worrying about the change.

I'm sure this whole thing will blow over soon.

I don't have any feelings about the change.

I just try to do what I have to do to get through

the day.

This doesn't really affect me.

It's not my responsibility.

Maybe someone will handle this for me.

It will go away.

It's not that bad.

I don't want to feel any pain or confusion.

The language of "Resistance"

I prefer the way things were before.

I don't know if I can do what is expected of me in this change.

I think this change is bad for the organization.

I feel angry about the change.

I can't concentrate on my work.

I'm upset about the way this whole thing has been happening.

Why me, why now?

I'll hide.

I won't listen.

I won't cooperate.

I'll blame someone else.

Language of **"Solutions and Acceptance"**

I'm excited about all the new possibilities the

change allows.

Everything is up in the air, but I'm dealing with the

real issues.

I keep thinking of new ways to do things.

The fear is lessening.

Recently I've had more energy to deal with change.

I'm learning new things.

I feel like the worst part of the change is over.

I feel more willing and cooperative.

My faith is now stronger than my fear.

I rather start seeking my options than be consumed

by fear.

I may not get what I want to happen but at least

I'll make an effort.

I'm feeling stronger and more confident.

I've really come a long way with this change.

It is…what it is.

I have mastered what needs to be done to be effective with this change.

I am comfortable in the new environment (work, city, relationship,)

I feel good about myself and what I have accomplished to meet the demands of the change.

I've learned things in this change that will help me deal with the next change.

I've made up my mind to survive and grow from this.

I'm glad that I'm taking more control of my life and making more decisions and taking more action.

My life will never be the same and yet I'm learning to move on with my life with a new awareness and new outlook on life. My life isn't over and I choose to begin again.

I'm not sure what's going to happen next, but I trust my God – my protection, my provision, my peace.

"It takes a lot of courage to release the familiar and seemingly secure, to embrace the new. But there is no real security in what is no longer meaningful. There is more security in the adventurous and exciting, for in movement there is life, and in change there is power."

~ Alan Cohen

"Change has the power to uplift, to heal, to stimulate, surprise, open new doors, bring fresh experience and create excitement in life. Certainly it is worth the risk. "

~ Leo Buscaglia

"The truth is that our finest moments are most likely to occur when we are feeling deeply uncomfortable, unhappy, or unfulfilled. For it is only in such moments, propelled by our discomfort, that we are likely to step out of our ruts and start searching for different ways or truer answers." ~ M. Scott Peck

"Everything must change. Nothing and no one remains the same." *~ popular song*

To everything there is a season, and a time to every purpose under heaven:
A time to be born, and a time to die;
A time to plant, and a time to pluck up that which is planted;
A time to kill, and a time to heal;
A time to break down, and a time to build up;
A time to weep, and a time to laugh;
A time to mourn, and time to dance;
A time to cast away stones, and a time to gather stones together;
A time to embrace, and a time to refrain from embracing . .
A time to love . . . *Ecclesiastes 3*

"To exist is to change, to change is to mature, to mature is to go on creating oneself endlessly."

~ Henri Bergson

"God grant me the serenity to accept the things I can not change, courage to change the things I can and the wisdom to know the difference."

~ Reinhold Niebuhr

Webster's definition of **"resilient"** is...

1. springing back; rebounding, returning to the original form or position after being bent,

2. compressed, or stretched, recovering readily from illness, depression, adversity, or the like; buoyant.

BE RESILIENT

In a harsh storm the palm tree bends instead of breaks.

After you have done all you can during your financial storm, health storm or relationships storm, just stand and be resilient. Bend but don't break. Be flexible and stay grounded in your faith. Remember, this, too, shall pass.

Don't allow the difficulty and disappointments to make your heart hard like a stone. Remember you are not alone.

"We are hard pressed on every side, yet not crushed; we are perplexed, but not in despair; persecuted, but not forsaken; struck down, but not destroyed." – II Corinthians 4:8-9

"Therefore we do not lose heart. Even though our outward man is being renewed day by day. For our light affliction, which is but for a moment, is working for us a far more exceeding and eternal weight of glory, while we do not look at the things which are seen, but at the things which are not seen. For the things which are seen are temporary, but the things which are not seen are eternal. " - II Corinthians 4:16-18

Think creatively and flexibly under stress. Remain connected to loved ones and important alliances rather than shut down when faced with a challenge.

Learn know how to mourn the inevitable losses in life. Know how to let go of things that you have no control over.

Look at adversity as a challenge rather than as a threat. Realize that no matter how the present situation turns out, you will learn and grow from it.

Resilience is one of the most important emotional intelligence coping skills you can have in today's fast-changing world. It means being able to bounce back after setbacks, failures, disappointments and losses. It means **not** giving up, and continuing to face the future with optimism, faith and courage despite the stress, sadness, storm, shifting, shaking and surprising events of life.

Your pain can change, however, faith requires patience.

Feeling rejected? Be resilient!

Feeling the anxiety of attacks from the enemy?
Be resilient.

Feeling tired and weary? Get inspired and be resilient!

Feeling lost in a wilderness of the unknown? Keep it moving. Don't give up. Stay in the light and be resilient !

Is your faith and purpose under fire? Remember the battle is not yours. Be resilient!

Experiencing loss and grief? Change is part of life. This, too, shall pass. You are still here. Be resilient and remember it is a choice to rejoice.

Have you been knocked down with criticism, abuse, injustice and overwhelming circumstances? Get up and be resilient! Reach out to others for help. Let go of pride, ego and fear. Find your voice.

Have you experienced setbacks in your finances, ministry or business? The recession will pass...be resilient! God is your provider.

 Have you lost your faith, joy, praise, gratitude, sense of humor, purpose and focus? **Bounce back and be resilient!**

Be sure to listen to my CD on how to be resilient during stressful times. This message of empowerment offers you 12 critical ways to be resilient. The CD is entitled "When You Fall... Let It Be on a Trampoline, not Concrete."

"See, I am doing a new thing!
Now it springs up; do you not perceive it?
I am making a way in the desert
and streams in the wasteland."

Isaiah 43:19 (NIV)

As you make room for God to do a new thing in your life, you must have the courage to do a "new thing" for yourself. Growth requires pressing, consistency, dedication, purpose and courage. Don't wait until you are sick and tired of being sick, tired, broke, lonely, stuck, abused, invisible, frustrated and desperate.

It's time to do a new thing!

If you have been quiet... it's time to speak up.

If you have been isolated and shy... it's time get out, socialize, network and meet new people.

If you have been a spender... it's time to be a saver.

If you have been discouraged... it's time to get up and be grateful.

If you have been a receiver, it's time to be a giver.

If you've been procrastinating... it's time to take action.

If you've been angry and holding a grudge, it's time to let go.

If you have never ventured beyond your local area... it's time to travel.

If you think it's too late for you...it's time to change your thinking and self-worth.

If you have been *stuck on stupid...* it's time to walk in wisdom and integrity.

If you have always been the giver... it's time learn how to receive.

If you seek escape and comfort in the wrong places, faces and things...it's time to learn how to cope in healthy and smarter ways.

If you receive invitations to gossip or argue...it's time to decline the invitation.

If you are always wearing your superwo(man) cape... it's time to delegate.

If you worry too much... it's time to start trusting God.

If you are always late and unorganized... it's time to start being punctual, organized and reliable.

If you have been prideful, closed and defensive... it's time to be teachable.

If you are afraid to learn how to drive, use the computer, learn a new language, travel, love again, go salsa dancing, start your own business, tell the grown children to move out, go on an audition or interview or find a new church home that really feeds your spirit, teaches the word of God and blesses the community... it's time to do a new thing!

If you have been running away from your ministry, ideas, talents and gifts... it's time to do a new thing!

It's time to let your light shine. There is a diamond inside of you. There is something precious inside of you. Your dreams, talents and God-given gifts are within you. In 2 Corinthians 4:7 we read about a treasure, but the treasure is kept in a jar of clay. We usually would keep our valuable treasures in a jewelry box, a vault, in a safety deposit box, or in a protected place. A jar of clay is fragile, and easily broken. A jar of clay reveals flaws, chips and cracks.

We are made from clay. We are ordinary and imperfect. A jar of clay is not a vessel of great worth or monetary value, but rather a common, ordinary vessel. You are that earthen vessel, that fragile cracked clay pot! God can do extraordinary things through ordinary  people (clay). The light and glory of God shines through the cracks of your earthen vessel. This is to remind us that our lives, our testimonies and our treasures within are important to reflect the glory and goodness of God. God wants to do a "new thing" in your life...but first you have to rid yourself of clutter, fear, limited thinking, low self-esteem, bitterness, poor choices and clinging to what is familiar, safe and comfortable. Ready...set...G R O W !

The 12 main issues to focus on to take my life to the next level are...

- ✓ **Decision making** – I will speak up.

- ✓ **Delays** – Procrastination is a thief. I will be proactive.

- ✓ **Doubt** – I believe in myself. I forgive myself. I trust myself to do the right thing.

- ✓ **Denial**– I open my mind, eyes and heart. I live in truth and peace.

- ✓ **Dedicated endurance** – I have faith, stamina and courage to grow through my difficulties.

- ✓ **Discipline** – I **keep** the main thing...the MAIN THING. I focus my attention on my intentions.

- ✓ **Dependencies** – I can let go of the emotional crutches. I can live without toxic people or substances. Day by day, I am feeling stronger.

- ✓ **Dead end relationships** – I value my life, my time, my body, my mind, my family and peace of mind. I deserve respect and love.

- ✓ **Depression** – I am **too** blessed to be stressed. Prayer changes things. God is able (Mark 9:23)

- ✓ **Debt** – I will create more avenues of income. I will save and spend wisely. I deserve the abundant life.

- ✓ **Diet** – I enjoy eating nutritious foods, drinking water and exercising my beautiful body. Health is my first wealth.

- ✓ **Disorganization** – I now reduce the weight of mental, emotional and physical clutter. I will de-clutter my mind, calendar and environment (i.e. anger, shame, old stuff, old clothes, office, closet, excess in activities, desk, car, purse, etc.)

Continue to train your brain for success with motivation, faith, knowledge and focused action. Books by motivational speaker and author **Jewel Diamond Taylor** are:

- **Sisterfriends**
- **Success Gems**
- **You Are Too Blessed to Be Stressed**
- **You Deserve More:** *Desperation is A* Terrible Perfume to Wear

To invite the speaker to your event, purchase books and CDs or to learn about upcoming speaking engagements, visit motivational web site

Visit web site - www.**DoNotGiveUp**.net

e-mail – JewelMotivates**@gmail**.com

or Jewel@DoNotGiveUp.net

call 323-964-1736

Jewel Diamond Taylor

4195 Chino Hills Pkwy

Chino Hills, CA 91709

Thank you for your business and the blessing of being of service to you. ~ Jewel Diamond Taylor

Notes